"Jesus never strutted knowledge. Mostly, he told subversive stories and asked piercing questions. David goes and does likewise. In *Reflections*, he brings to the task a knack for both story and question, and—like Jesus—reveals the heart's hidden workings."

~ *Mark Buchanan, author and pastor*

"*Reflections* is a journey for anyone who wants to engage in the rewarding pilgrimage of walking honestly and transparently with God in the messy business of being human. David does a great job, openly sharing his own road. It's compelling!"

~ *Dr. Tom Cooper, president, City In Focus*

"I like going deeper with real life issues and with people! In *Reflections*, David Collins is honest and frank, thought provoking. Here is a man seeking to have open encounters with the living God. *Reflections* prepares my heart and soul to hear the Truth and live the Truth with Jesus."

~ *Dr. Hal W. Hadden, founder and CEO, Christian Leadership Concepts*

"Herein, we find grand old concepts, like 'walking in the Spirit' and 'following Jesus' made flesh. In David's gentle, Jesus way, he takes us by the hand and walks us through a journey where we might not dare go ourselves. Real life—fragmented, messy, mysterious—lived in response to and alongside real God. This is so much more than a devotional book. This is the real deal that can make us the real deal."

~ *Brad Jersak, Fresh Wind, pastor, author*

D0807846

"I have known Dave Collins for nearly a quarter of a century. I will never forget the first time I heard him speak. His insights, gift with words, and storytelling captured my imagination. David is a man who lives his life transparently. He is on a journey, a grand adventure. He has allowed me to walk with him over the years. Or perhaps it is better to say that he has drawn me into his journey.

In *Reflections*, David is creating a way for others to walk with him and the One who leads him on this pilgrimage toward the City of God. David's gifts in speaking have been transformed into writing. *Reflections* will not let you walk passively. It will draw you into David's journey in a way that will challenge you to reflect on your own. Consider yourself fairly warned; if you pick up this book, be prepared to be changed."

~ *Darrow L. Miller, co-founder, Disciple Nations Alliance; author, teacher*

"I loved walking with David Collins in *Reflections*. He transparently invites the reader to join him in sensitive areas of life's journey. His thoughts are fresh, provocative, and they invite the reader to consider the same questions for their journey. The book is divided into chapters that lend themselves to a series of daily readings. My favorite chapters are Hope and Longings. I wonder what yours will be? Be prepared to identify, to be challenged, and to tear up and chuckle with recognition."

~ *Dr. Bob Moffitt, founding president & CEO, The Harvest Foundation; author*

"Many 'nuggets' are hidden in these pages, awaiting the opening of heart and soul of those seeking real treasure."

~ *William Young, author of* The Shack

reflections

david collins

Illustrated by: Cam Cardow

forever books
WINNIPEG, CANADA
www.foreverbooks.ca

Reflections: Holiness ~ Wholeness

Copyright © 2010

All Rights Reserved. No part of this publication may be reproduced, stored in a retrieval system or transmitted in any form or by any means—electronic, mechanical, photocopy, recording or any other—except for brief quotations in printed reviews, without the prior permission of the author.

ISBN: 978-1-926718-09-5

All Scripture quotations, unless otherwise indicated are taken from the Holy Bible, New Living Translation, © 1996, 2004. Used by permission of Tyndale House Publishers, Inc., Wheaton, Illinois 60189. All rights reserved.

Scripture quotations, marked "NIV" are taken from the Holy Bible, New International Version®. Copyright © 1973, 1978, 1984 International Bible Society. Used by permission of Zondervan Bible Publishers."

Scripture quotations marked "NCV" are taken from the New Century Version, Thomas Nelson Publishers, ©1991

Illutrations on pages 100, 127 and 134 are used with the permission of Cam Cardow. All other illustrations are used with permission by Caglecartoons.com.

Photos on pages 18 and 76 are used with the permission of Lindsay Brucks.

Photo of back of author's head on page 143 is used with the permission of Peter Mogan.

All other photos are used with the permission of David Collins.

Cover Design: Yvonne Parks Design

Book Design: Andrew Mackay

Managing Editor: Rick Johnson

Printed in Canada.

Published by

Forever Books

WINNIPEG CANADA
www.foreverbooks.ca

Dedication

To each who is searching to know their Creator and to those who have walked with me through my own journey; specifically my most faithful friend, Nancy; and my children, who received the brunt of my maturing process:
Melody, Nathan, Angela and Elyeese.

Acknowledgments

When dialoguing with God about this book, I asked, "Why write something that has already been written and that no one will read?" His answer was simply, "Who said anyone had to read it?" I am most thankful for that release.

It is also important to thank each person who spoke the query, "Have you written this down in a book?" It became a dreaded question but also a gentle prod.

The Oikodome Foundation, with its purposeful commitment to the influencing of ideas, has made the printing of this book possible. Virginia, Walter and Lyle's edits gave it a semblance of order.

And, of course there are the idea shapers in my own life: Teo, Darrow, Bob, Keith, Dave—with scores of others who were courageous enough to consider ideas that did not conform to the norm. They helped to open the door of mystery and enabled me to see God as one beyond my understanding, and still feel safe in his presence.

Cam, you helped me display these concepts visually.

Contents

Preface to the Reflections Series

With all my heart I want your blessings. Be merciful as you promised. I pondered the direction of my life, and I turned to follow your laws (Psalm 119: 58, 59).

I am a man under the weight of authority. The weight says, "Don't screw up." When GOD speaks, he removes the weight. It always boils down to trust. Do I trust him enough to honestly believe him? When I do, it ultimately improves my day. Yet there remains a conscious gap between these two worlds: Performance and Peace.

This journey of sharing my reflections, God intended for my benefit. It is my place of discovery, my place of longing—a place that discovers Jesus the Christ for myself. It may be of help to you because we find more common ground in our places of suffering than in our places of success.

These reflections are the story of my struggles and where I have found peace.

I have begun to hear the voice of God speaking words of affirmation.

"I cherish you. I am proud of you. I know you by name and value my time with you. I know your weaknesses and accept them as part of who you are. I have no intention of trying to make you conform. You can't do anything that will cause me to love you less. Nor can you do anything that will cause me to love you more. You are special the way you are."

11

Reflections

Early in life, I was told about a God like that. Through the years, experience has proven that to be true. Whether I was in a crowd, alone, in a wilderness environment; whenever God revealed himself to me in deeply intimate ways, it was always one-on-one. He spoke to me, drew me closer and I knew I wanted more.

My life is not a summation of my activity. The choices available to me have been limitless. Had I made different decisions at any of life's critical junctures, my life would be significantly different. The "might-have-beens" are easy to imagine. Second-guessing, however, is not usually productive.

Reflection is a frightening place for some. It can open wounds that have only recently scabbed over. Scars may be revealed that we have spent years concealing. Some places of our lives may still be too painful to journey to. That's okay. At midlife, I stumbled into a major truth about myself. God, in his sovereignty, knew when I was ready to process that information and apply it.

The telling of my story had become routine for me. I grew up speaking Vietnamese in an isolated fishing village in Vietnam. I wasn't aware that I was white until I was five, but realization told me that I was somehow different.

I entered boarding school not being able to recognize the letters of the alphabet. A few weeks into the semester found me placed in the dumb class. They called it "special". We all understood it meant "dumb".

It took almost 50 years before I realized for the first time that English had been my second language. At fifty-two, my reality changed with that one insight. What I had come to believe early on in my life was profoundly altered. It was no longer an issue of whether I was dumb. It was simply a reality in circumstance. I had grown up hating languages, hating reading. Now I had a sudden realization of lost years and wasted opportunity. Now I also had new horizons to explore and consider. More importantly, I had something to write about.

Reflections for the Journey

This is a journey we are on together. Within these pages I offer a series of observations and invite you to explore your own reflections. Do you feel you need permission to begin to explore the private places of your soul? What is the insight you have to gain from telling your story again?

Preface to the Reflections Series

Each "reflection" is an invitation to wholeness and holiness. If you haven't ventured along this road before, let that journey begin now. If you know this road well, may your reflections affirm the truths you are gleaning as you persist in your journey.

We need never grow tired or fearful of discovery. So I invite you into reflection by sharing my thoughts and questions, my dreams and fears. It will take us to the end of life to understand our true motivations and fully welcome being drawn into the mystery of God.

Wholeness
Chapter One

The Kingdom of Heaven is like a treasure that a man dis-
covered hidden in a field. In his excitement, he hid it
again and sold everything he owned to get enough
money to buy the field (Matthew 13:44).

My life has been more a quest than a religious journey. On this quest, I have discovered that simplistic answers are worse than frustrating. They are like scoops of ice cream dropped on the sidewalk after one lick of the cone—so much potential, but they leave you with nothing.

I want the whole scoop. I want to suck every drop out the end of the cone and then eat the cone too. Please don't feed me pat answers and don't ask me to just believe. I have an insatiable need to understand why.

Jesus spoke of the Kingdom of God being like a man who discovered a treasure buried in a field. Without telling anyone, the man sold all he had and purchased the field. Whenever that story has been told to me it seemed to always be in the context of sacrifice. He sold everything.

I missed the most critical point.

Everything that man possessed was worth less than the treasure he knew he would gain. It wasn't about loss. It was about a shrewd investment! There is more buried in that field than you can see, but even what you see is enough to convince you that this is worth more than everything you own. The realization is of riches that far exceed your expectations.

A man who had been sick for thirty-eight years spent his life beside a pool. It was believed the Spirit of God would visit that place, stir up the waters, and heal the first person to enter. Did it ever occur? Who knows.

> *When Jesus asked, "Do you want to be well?" he was asking, "Do you want to be whole?"*

Jesus did however ask this man, "Would you like to get well?" (Read John 5.)

He did not ask, "Do you want to be healed?" If this man were truly to become well, his whole life would change, not just his body. He would no longer have a reason to show up at a pool and beg. His caregivers might find themselves out of a job. His friends had defined their relationship with him through the lens of his inability. He would have to learn a trade and start to support himself.

When Jesus asked, "Do you want to be well?" he was asking, "Do you want to be whole?"

This story stirs something in my own soul about wholeness. There have been many places and times throughout my life when I have not felt whole. I have felt broken, insignificant, inferior, incomplete, fearful and at times, incompetent. I have spent many hours waiting for the rippling of waters. If I could just get in first… If I could just get that break…

I wonder what wellness would look like if I truly realized it in all aspects of my life—not just in my physical health? What would it mean to choose to live well? To be whole?

As I reflected on the question Jesus asked this man, my soul understood its implication.

The complaining stops. The blame, the anger, resentment and accusations cease. I want to choose wellness. Yes, I want to be whole in all aspects of my life.

Reflections for the Journey

Jesus' invitation is extended to you. "Would you like to get well?" Do you want it enough? Are you desperate enough to release the crutches in your life that you have come to trust?

Take a moment to consider your places of dependency. Who do you rely upon? Which voices do you listen to? What does security look like to you?

Parable of the Growing Seed

Jesus also said: "The Kingdom of God is like a farmer who scatters seed on the ground. Night and day, while he's asleep or awake, the seed sprouts and grows, but he does not understand how it happens. The earth produces the crops on its own. First a leaf blade pushes through, then the heads of wheat are formed, and finally the grain ripens. And as soon as the grain is ready, the farmer comes and harvests it with a sickle, for the harvest time has come."

Parable of the Mustard Seed

Jesus said: "How can I describe the Kingdom of God? What story should I use to illustrate it? It is like a mustard seed planted in the ground. It is the smallest of all seeds, but it becomes the largest of all garden plants; it grows long branches and birds can make nests in its shade" (Mark 4:26–32).

Reflections

Even in war, we can laugh at our mistakes.

"Quit"

Chapter Two

"So what do people get in this life for all their hard work and anxiety? Their days of labor are filled with pain and grief; even at night their minds cannot rest. It is all meaningless" (Ecclesiastes 2:22–23).

Quit what?

"Quit trying."

Quit trying to do what?

"Quit trying to be a Christian."

What? Are you insane? Do you know what people are going to say if they hear me say that? Do you know what could happen? They'll say I've betrayed my faith. And what if they're right? What if I end up denying that you exist at all? You want me to quit? I don't know you. You are not the package I have been sold my entire life. You are supposed to be predictable. How can you ask me to quit? I have to do my part. I have to do your will. I have to be holy like you are holy. You even said so yourself.

"Walk with me."

I don't know how.

"Try putting one foot ahead of the other. Don't look way down the trail. Start with just one foot in front of the other."

But where are we going?

"Does it matter?"

Of course it matters! What if I go to the wrong place? What if I don't go where I am supposed to go? What if I mess up everything by wandering off?

"If you are wandering off with me, can you really mess up? How wrong can you be if I am walking with you?"

You don't know what others say about me or might say.

"Which is it? What others say? Or, what others might say?"

A bit of both, I guess. I've had one or two who thought I was a bit heretical.

"Are they the norm?"

No. But I fear what others might say.

"How much of your life do you live in fear of what other's might say?"

A lot, actually.

"Why do you think that is?"

> What if I told you
> that you didn't need
> to do anything to
> be special?

Because I want them to like me. I want to be valued. I want people to think that I am wise and smart. I want to feel like I am good at something and that my life has meaning. That I am good enough to be special.

"What if I told you that you didn't need to do anything to be special? What if I could help you believe that you are special because I made you that way?"

I don't know. I have spent my whole life believing that I had to measure up. What do I do if I don't have to prove my significance?

"Try putting one foot ahead of your other one."

That's it! That's all you're going to tell me? I need to know what I need to do. I need to know where I am going. I need to know the expectations that I have to fulfill so that I don't screw it up and end up looking foolish or worse, stupid, incompetent, immature—just ordinary David—nobody special.

"How far down the road did you just run? I can hardly see you you're so far away. From my vantage point, you are already down in that far away valley and you ran there all by yourself, alone. You can't see Me there because I didn't walk with you there."

"Quit"

I just want to please you. I just want to know I am doing it right. I don't want to have more failure in my life.

"You seem to be focused on your inabilities, your failures, your fears, your needs, your wants, your achievements, your recognition, your value ... Do you notice the one thing these all have in common?"

Cut it out! That's not fair. Don't twist what I say. I am trying to please you. I am trying to live the Christian life. I want to be a good follower of Jesus. Don't make light of my pain and don't make light of my effort.

"That's good. Get it out."

God ... you're supposed to correct me. You're supposed to tell me that I am not to question you; that it is sacrilege to talk to you like this. You're supposed to do the Charlton Heston thing on the mountain—booming voice of God shouting, "Thou Shalt Not Mess With God!"

"I love you David. I love you just the way you are. I love your brokenness. I love your struggle, even when it took you to sin. I love your heart and the genuine desire to know me. I love your confusion that resulted in your chasing down roads that left you dirty and sometimes bleeding. Ultimately, you dead-ended in places where you knew you needed to retrace your steps back to this place."

And where is this place exactly?

"It is where I AM."

Oh God ... I am afraid of this place. It is a place that I cannot manipulate. It is holy. In this place I have no pretense. You know me here. I am dirty. The pedestals I have stood on are cheap trinkets and the praises of others have a putrid smell. God, in this place I am nothing.

"David, my son. You are my beloved son, in whom I am well pleased."

Look at me! I am filth. My whole attention is in self-absorption. My whole life has been all about me. How can you say you are pleased with me?

"Do you honestly believe that I do not know who you are? I formed you in your mother's womb. I knit you together. I know the plans I have for you David. They are not plans to harm and destroy. They are plans to bring healing and wholeness. No eye has seen. No ear has heard. No one has ever conceived what I have in store for you. You are my cherished possession. I love you with an everlasting love. I have always loved you. When you longed to be held, to be noticed, to be valued and cherished, I loved you.

Reflections

"Some in the spirit world do not. Some have intended to hurt you, wound you, break you. That will not happen. I AM has been with you even when you could not see and your ears could not hear. Your brokenness will become your greatest strength."

Reflections for the Journey

Have you ever stopped to realize that you have no secrets? Nothing about you surprises God. His love for you is not conditioned to your response to him. He loves you regardless of how you treat him. If you obey him completely, he will not love you more than he has always loved you. His love is perfect. It is everlasting.

Such love has no fear, because perfect love expels all fear. If we are afraid, it is for fear of punishment, and this shows that we have not fully experienced his perfect love. We love each other because he loved us first"
(1 John 4:18–19).

I AM
Chapter Three

God said to Moses, *"I am who I am. Say this to the people of Israel: I Am has sent me to you"* (Exodus 3:14).

Is this a riddle? I know the answers... "All things work together for good to..."

"David. I AM the answer. It isn't the text. What you have read is living and active. It is sharper than a two-edged sword. It can separate the bone from its marrow. I AM knows the thoughts and intentions of your heart. Let go of the answers David."

It is a riddle.

"No. It's a journey. A journey isn't so much about the destination as it is the experience itself. I AM mystery. I AM wonder. I AM your companion, your friend, your lover..."

Wait a minute. That's a little too intimate for me. Don't go there.

"I AM already there. I have loved you with an undying love. Get over it. Realize it. Accept it. It isn't so much about you as it is about me. This is my choice. It does not depend upon your willingness to accept it."

Yes it does. If I don't submit and pray the prayer, I don't get in. I end up a "goat" instead of a "sheep". You know what I'm talking about. The prayer! "Oh God, I am a sinner. Please forgive me. I ask Jesus into my heart. Amen." Sound familiar?

Reflections for the Journey

Where do we begin with God?

> I have loved you with an undying love. Get over it. Realize it. Accept it. It isn't so much about you as it is about me.

"O God, You are my starting point. Free me to begin with you. Enable me to release what I cannot bear. Strengthen me in belief, to trust the words you say. Be my starting place today."

"In Him we live and move and exist..." (Acts 17:28a).

Salvation

Chapter Four

The greatest theological concept I have ever heard:
"Jesus loves me, this I know." ~ Carl Barth, theologian

A favorite song in my youth was "Stairway to Heaven". I had no idea what they were singing about but I did know that it made for a wonderfully long, slow dance. It conjured up images of Jacob sleeping in the desert, dreaming of exactly that, a stairway to heaven. What kind of teenage kid thinks about stories from Sunday School when dancing with a pretty girl? I knew it was a quantum stretch of the imagination to force that much spirituality into a song, especially that song, but I needed a defense to rationalize the fact that I was dancing (but that is another issue).

"David, when did your salvation begin?"

When I said the prayer.

"So is salvation something you did? Or is salvation something I did?"

…You did.

"When did your salvation begin David?"

You tell me.

"Before you were born, I chose you. You know the word 'predestined' from Bible College days. And it is true. I created you with a longing for me. I did not interfere with the decisions you were making nor did I place a hedge of protection around you

25

so that you would be sheltered. But each longing of your heart created a vacuum. It moved you to attempt to fill it. Your efforts fell short. You kept trying and I continued to allow circumstance and individuals into your life that increased your capacity to understand.

"David, you have had an ever-expanding capacity to know me from the moment of your conception. With each new level of understanding came a new level of redemption in your life, until one day, you were able to comprehend that you needed ME."

What are you saying? Is everybody on this trajectory? Everybody is "being saved"?

"David, I AM the one who knows the thoughts and intentions of each heart. I know the ones who openly reject what I have offered. But this you also must remember. I AM not willing that any perish. Some will say that they knew me, that they served me, but they know, and I know, that they only served themselves. Each person is responsible for the choices he or she makes. You leave the fate of others to me. You have much to think about."

We are creatures of justification. I have always known that a ticket to heaven was a lot better than a free fall into hell. That was reason enough to pray "the sinner's prayer" and make sure that my eternity was safeguarded.

The fear of hell and promise of heaven were my primary motivators to become a follower of Jesus the Christ. A perfect example of a profound truth being reduced to a simplistic explanation. God's intervention in history was Christ's invitation to move in with him, sit down, shed the shoes from our swollen feet and rest. The focal point is not a demarcation of who is in and who is out. Rather it is a pronouncement of adoption into a family, God's family. It is not a membership in a club. It was and remains a position of inclusion for all who want it, rather than fear of exclusion for breaking the club's rules.

> *"So is salvation something you did? Or is salvation something I did?"*

A Biblical summary of the salvation story recognizes that the Creator of everything that exists (seen and unseen) willingly entered history, became like one of us, endured every form of temptation without succumbing, and ultimately died and rose again to restore his creation to its original intent. (Read Colossians 1:15–20.) That statement implies something far greater than an escape clause from hell.

Salvation

Life choices have consequences. Jesus had very little tolerance for those who took advantage of others or valued themselves above others. He leveled the playing field as he cleared the temple of people who swindled the less fortunate. Even in his death, the temple curtain that divided the holy place from the common person was torn open. The most sacred place suddenly became available to everyone. Women and children, beggars and merchants, all are invited into relationship with God.

I struggle with the club mentality of religion. "When did you become a member? We would like to know the time and place. Do you have credentials? It is us and them and our job is to get them to become one of us."

> *Somehow, I lost sight of the fact I will always be a "them."*

Somehow, I lost sight of the fact that I will always be a "them".

For many, these are uncharted waters. Is salvation more than a line in the sand that I stepped across by saying a simple prayer? What is its benefit and how is it received?

Salvation is God enabling me to know him. It is having my original purpose restored. It begins in my life before I am aware of it and draws me to a point where I must decide whether to submit to it or not. It's done. It's over. It's finished in a literal act of sacrifice by Christ, once and for all. But do I want it?

God accomplished it. I'm learning to progressively receive more of it. It becomes the lens through which I am now able to increasingly see all of life as God intended it to be. My perceptions are adjusting. It is a metamorphosis that pleases me, even though I still cannot imagine its full implications. It is a life-long discovery.

My life is an unmarked box filled with puzzle pieces, dumped out. God links one to another. Initially there is no perception or comprehension of what that picture looks like. It's scattered. It's messy. I may try to prevent God from sliding one piece into the next. It can be disorderly, with well-intentioned people trying to force pieces into wrong slots. They don't fit.

Many religions view all others in this category. There is an assumption that Christ's transformation begins with our verbal commitment to submit to him. The reality however, is that God is always at work in the lives of every individual, even while we are still in the womb of our mothers. Our capacity to know him continually expands. With each decision, a choice is being made to follow or not follow the ways of God. The last puzzle piece drops into place when eternity begins.

Throughout life, we are individually prompted by the Spirit of God to live fully. We have seen his design in creation and have no excuses. (Read Romans 1:18–32.) As our comprehension increases, the more intentional are our decisions to surrender and submit to, or reject, the God who is revealing himself to us.

One decision alone didn't make me a member of the heaven-bound club. I make decisions multiple times a day to follow Christ. Some might wonder if this implies the need to "be saved" multiple times. That train of thought misses the point. It is not an issue of saved or unsaved. It is an issue of acceptance or rejection; loving obedience or disobedience. If I do all the right things with the wrong motive, will it be of any benefit to me? Many will stand before Christ and say, "We performed all these actions in your name." Christ's response will be, "I never knew you."

Jesus spoke about people who believed salvation was simply a statement we make, the prayer without consequence, the action without the loving submission. He warned that many will be surprised by who is in heaven and who is not. (Read Matthew 25:31–46.)

It is a tragic reality that the gift of salvation has been reduced by many to a level of personal achievement.

"I have prayed the prayer and I am in."

"The good things I do balance out the bad."

It is a sad heresy with serious consequence.

One of my greatest surprises was the realization that every decision I make ultimately is a response to Christ. If harshly criticized, do I respond in similar fashion, or am I tempered by my willingness to see each individual through the lens of God? How do I observe the tragic condition of the needy? Will I treat each casual acquaintance with dignity? How sensitive am I to the environment that God loves? Each is a decision to submit to the will of God or resist. Salvation enables my capacity to increasingly choose the wiser road.

Salvation is my choice to receive. Salvation is also the work of God in me, enabling me to understand more fully the benefit of living well in all areas of life. In doing so, I bring Christ pleasure.

Reflections for the Journey

You are more competent now in many areas of life than you were ten years ago. How has your relationship with God evolved over that same period of time?

———

When I was a child, I spoke and thought and reasoned as a child. But when I grew up, I put away childish things. Now we see things imperfectly as in a cloudy mirror, but then we will see everything with perfect clarity. All that I know now is partial and incomplete, but then I will know everything completely, just as God now knows me completely. Three things will last forever— faith, hope, and love—and the greatest of these is love (1 Corinthians 13:11–13).

———

He is the kind of high priest we need because he is holy and blameless, unstained by sin. He has been set apart from sinners and has been given the highest place of honor in heaven. Unlike those other high priests, he does not need to offer sacrifices every day. They did this for their own sins first and then for the sins of the people. But Jesus did this once for all when he offered himself as the sacrifice for the people's sins. The law appointed high priests who were limited by human weakness. But after the law was given, God appointed his Son with an oath, and his Son has been made the perfect High Priest forever (Hebrews 7:26–28).

———

"Jesus answered, 'I tell you the truth, no one can enter the kingdom of God unless he is born of water and the Spirit. Flesh gives birth to flesh, but the Spirit gives birth

to spirit. You should not be surprised at my saying you must be born again. The wind blows wherever it pleases. You hear its sound, but you cannot tell where it comes from or where it is going. So it is with everyone born of the Spirit… (21). But whoever lives by the truth comes into the light, so that it may be seen plainly that what he has done has been done through God' " (John 3:5–8, 21 NIV).

Stillness

Chapter Five

Be still, and know that I am God! I will be honored by every nation. I will be honored throughout the world (Psalm 46:10).

*C*ome away. Come to a lonely place."
I don't know LORD. Don't I have enough loneliness in my life? Isn't that the great struggle of my heart?

"When I was pursued by the masses, I knew my limits. I also knew where my strength comes from. I only did what My Father showed me to do. I only spoke what he told me to say. I learned to commune with him. I both learned and experienced it in the lonely place."

Doesn't personality have something to do with this? Aren't some people more prone to being quiet, seeking solitude, enjoying isolation?

"Most people struggle being alone with themselves."

How does a person get to know God? It seems an endless pursuit that has its moments of wonderful intimacy and times of dark despair. Yet Scripture always comes back to one central point when contemplating God's response to humanity. It is always the invitation.

Reflections

"Come away with me. Be with me." My training said that meant "having devotions every day."

Have you ever failed at having devotions every day; that time of intentional Bible study and prayer? That has to be on my all time list of failed New Year's resolutions. In the failing to be consistent came a bolstering of my own sense of failure, my own disappointing God.

It is an ugly trap to fall into. It is the self-reinforced prophecy. "You have nothing special to offer, therefore you are nothing special." So you try to be someone special through your commitment to a task. When you don't produce, you realize that it must be true, and you settle for mediocrity—strange.

> *Most people struggle being alone with themselves.*

Jesus invites us to come. *"Come to Me, all who are weary…"* I'm weary.

"Come all who are weighed down…" I'm weighed down.

"And I will give you rest."

I am more introverted than extraverted. Yet being alone with myself did not come naturally. I gravitate to distraction. It can be the television, a computer game, a drive to the store and even mindless wandering, but always busy. As soon as I am left alone, my first reaction has historically been to busy myself. Culture has befriended busyness and consumption.

In the backdrop, Jesus invites me to come away and be with him. Alone. Without distraction.

Do you feel the uneasiness of that? Any sense of panic yet?

Okay, let's try it for an hour. So it takes me twenty minutes to prepare, five minutes to answer the phone; eight minutes to send that email I forgot to get out; four minutes to re-settle and, before I know it, I have managed to eat up an hour without being alone.

Bill Lane says, "Our age is a dialogue of the deaf." In other words, we don't know how to listen.

God on the other hand says:

"Be still."

"Be still and know."

Stillness

"Be still and know that I AM God."

"Be still. I will be exalted among the nations.

"Be still. I will be exalted in the earth."

~ Psalms 46:10 (Paraphrase)

I have never been a "still" kind of person. Wasteful, yes; but not still.

It started with one day. One day dedicated to being with God. Just hanging out together. I had no idea what to expect except that I had a deep conviction that it was time. I took my Bible, a pad of paper, pen and a six-hour block.

It turned out better than I expected, but truth be told, I didn't know what to expect. I became so tired, I fell asleep. Waking an hour later, I did the math on what that nap cost the company, based on my hourly rate. My first reaction was a feeling of guilt for my lack of productivity, followed by God's directive to just accept it as a gift.

"You were tired. You slept. I made you that way. Now notice the surroundings. There is more for you to enjoy."

Self-accusation is always quick to express its point.

A lesson learned; communing without an agenda prepares the soul to listen. Read your Bible when you have an expectancy to discover. There isn't a required quota. You may only finish part of a sentence before you realize that a clear statement has been made. What did it honestly say? Record it. Record what you heard God say from his Word during your time of quiet refection. Write down each insight he reveals.

Sometimes you will hear something that sounds more like heresy than doctrine. "God, you can't mean that. That goes against everything I have been taught."

Write it down.

> *Self-accusation is always quick to express its point.*

The invitation to *"come away and be with me,"* is not given to reinforce what you already know. The invitation is to discover what you don't yet know and allow yourself the privilege of holding it, turning it around and looking at it. Taste it, reflect upon it. Chew it and digest it. Ask your questions and always be listening for the answer.

Reflections

"Come away with me, to a lonely place. I have something to tell you. Don't fear it. Don't try to define it. Resist controlling or limiting it. You are safe with me."

Reflections for the Journey

Do I know how to be still?

Mystery
Chapter Six

O LORD, you ... know everything about me ... Such knowledge is too wonderful for me, too great for me to understand (Psalm 139:1, 6)!

What I once feared has now become the attribute I most love. I have moved from always needing to understand God to a place where I deeply cherish the mystery of God. It is a good thing to not fully comprehend your Creator; to wonder about his nature and attributes; to not be able to explain the circumstances of life with ease.

Journeying is different than a trip. A trip has clear boundaries, objectives, outcomes and destination in mind. I thought God wanted me to take a trip with him.

I compare religion to a trip; faith to a journey. I hated the trip. It was empty. There were the moments of color and pleasure, but the mystery was not there. It was predictable to the point that I could tell you what God was like. I could tell you the answers to almost any circumstance. Do you need help? Here are three steps you can take to get you through. Life was prescribed and sterile. And so was God.

Was this the one to whom I should commit my life and soul? He has no power. He has no flavor. He is bland, familiar. I can never meet his expectations and rarely sense his pleasure. I understand him. He's ... like me. This can't be GOD.

Where there is mistrust of the mystery of God, there will be walls to protect against it. The orderliness of life has been our safe place. It can be defined.

> *Without mystery and personal revelation, theology becomes sterile*

The Presence of God and what he might do is not so easily defined. Even more unsettling is the thought of what he may do to us and through us. We have become accustomed to the prescribed ways in which God speaks and how to appropriately respond to him.

Knowing God is dependent upon what he chooses to reveal about himself. The invitation is to come to him. *"Come to me, all of you who are weary and carry heavy burdens, and I will give you rest"* (Matthew 11:28).

"Abide in me, like I abide in my Father. As I am united with him, so you are united with me." (Read John 15.)

Pursuing that intimacy has found me in churches, attending courses, reading books—listening to what others have learned about God. The truth is that we can know much about God from numerous sources, but you can only know God through his own revelation to you. I did not realize there was a difference until God's word began to speak to me without the assistance of friends, pastors or authors (not bad in themselves, simply not the source).

Paul, the apostle, prayed that God will *"give you a spirit of wisdom and revelation, so that you will have full knowledge of him. He will give light to the eyes of your hearts, so that you will understand the hope to which he has called you. You will begin to discover the rich inheritance he has promised and how his power works in you in ways beyond what you ever conceived possible because you trust him."* (Read Ephesians 1:16–22.)

Mystery, wonder, contradiction, doubt, turmoil, struggle, weariness, fear, surrender, healing, rest, mystery. "God, who are we that you are even aware of us?"

Mystery has led me to believe that I have relied too heavily on others' descriptions of God. Theology is a wonderful word that opens great insights. Yet without mystery and personal revelation, theology becomes sterile, religious and, eventually, only form.

"But isn't there a risk of heresy? Shouldn't we put up some safeguards?"

What does Scripture tell you? Why do we fear releasing people into the hands of God? Open avenues that encourage intimacy with God and spend less time attempting to protect God from us. Sharing those discoveries with others maintains a healthy level of accountability.

Oh, the mystery and wonder of God. Who can know it?

Reflections for the Journey

Have you ever experienced hearing the voice of God speaking directly to you? Although you may not naturally gravitate to times of solitude, recognize their importance. If this is a new practice, begin gradually with an hour in a place where you will not be disturbed or distracted. Go without an agenda. Simply record whatever it is you sense God is saying; nothing more. Do not worry if it seems disconnected and fragmented. This time is dedicated to simply listening, recording, and reflecting. Blank pages are completely acceptable.

Fragments
Chapter Seven

*Experiences spill into each other as we bring our world
to the table and try to sort through the tangles.*

My experiences in Rwanda during the final days of the 1994 genocide still live in my thoughts. I watched people barely holding on to the remaining fragments of their lives. I sat on a wall overlooking a courtyard where

Surviving with the remnants of the Rwandan Genocide 1994

women brought their weaving, hoping for a sale. On the opposite side of that wall was a mass grave where their relatives lay buried, some of them incompletely.

Traveling to the refugee camps across the border in Eastern Congo, a young boy passed me. A deep machete scar from one cheekbone to the other left an eighth-inch gap through the bridge of his nose.

A little baby and her two older sisters were the only survivors in their family. I asked the little girl's name. Everyone Hates Me was the name given by her mother before her own death.

Three weeks of repeated tragedy. No sense of reason and little hope. A flood of emotions would sweep over me as I walked with victims, and also murderers. Through it all, I was unable to shed a tear.

Routed through Brussels on my return flight, the airline put me up in a hotel. To get there I had to travel by train, then walk through a red light district. I wasn't ready. These were beautiful women, seductively dressed. Not in a sleazy way. They were more elegant, with gentleness about them. They said the very words my soul longed to hear.

"You look exhausted. Do you need someone to talk to? Do you need someone to hold you tonight?"

I'm not sure how I managed to arrive at my room alone that night. My whole being ached for some semblance of sanity, compassion, gentleness and, yes, love. I told God that if this is what relief work was going to be like, I didn't think I could handle it.

> *Life is not made up of tidy, self-contained compartments.*

A few months later found me preaching on the first Sunday of the month. In many evangelical traditions, that is Communion Sunday. On this occasion, the communion service preceded the sermon. Hymn after hymn seemed to be about blood. "There is a fountain filled with blood..."

I could see it. Blood everywhere, death, suffering, pain, terror. I lost it on the front pew. I wept my first tears. No one knew that a dam had burst in my soul, allowing a lifetime of pain (others' mostly) to flood out of me.

Life is not made up of tidy, self-contained compartments. Experiences spill into each other as we bring our world, full of every emotion, to the table and try to sort through the tangles.

Reflections

Even when we say we value a certain level of order and harmony in our lives, we also have the capacity to sabotage it. We can hold onto resentments, regrets and excuses because they provide us with a sense of permission to remain dysfunctional or handicapped. Ironically, bitterness can be valued to a greater degree than reconciliation. Anger can be seen as more principled than forgiveness.

The experiences of our lives are all connected. Our work influences our perceptions about ourselves. Times of leisure refresh us and build strength for times of drain. Our spiritual life permeates them all. Everything we do affects us in some way. Some experiences are messy. Some are filled with pain. Others give meaning to words like beauty, peace, hope and love.

Time has allowed me to see the places of connection that can be overlooked.

Reflections for the Journey

Remember a defining moment when your life was shaped by a word of encouragement or criticism. How old were you? What mark has been placed in your life because of it?

I am the vine; you are the branches. If a man remains in me and I in him, he will bear much fruit; apart from me you can do nothing (John 15:5 NIV).

Don't use foul or abusive language. Let everything you say be good and helpful, so that your words will be an encouragement to those who hear them. And do not bring sorrow to God's Holy Spirit by the way you live. Remember, he has identified you as his own, guaranteeing that you will be saved on the day of redemption. Get rid of all bitterness, rage, anger, harsh words, and slander, as well as all types of evil behavior (Ephesians 4:29–31).

Giftedness
Chapter Eight

"Whoso knoweth himself well, is lowly in his own sight and delights not in the praises of men... Be not therefore extolled in thine own mind for any art or science which thou knowest, but rather let the knowledge given thee make thee more humble and cautious."
~ Thomas à Kempis, *Imitation of Christ*

Three individuals had ten minutes to ask me any questions they wished. They had known me for three days. Their written assignment was to describe the strengths they perceived in me. Their conclusions were remarkably similar. The qualities they listed were also values and characteristics of importance to me. How were they able to discern who I was after such a short time?

As a teenager, I was intrigued by the idea that God had given me a special gift. We each hoped to discover that ours was somehow "superior" to the rest. Surveys were taken and some people seemed to shine. My results lacked the luster.

My senior year of high school found me in a boarding environment in Malaysia, with extremely gifted roommates. They were the athletes, the scholars, the leaders, the ... maybe a few other things. Next to them, I felt like a faded dishcloth. The best I could hope for was: "You're good with little kids."

Good with little kids. It seemed to fall short in a high school's list of distinguished achievements. Yet the years have been good, assisting me to understand the uniqueness of my gifting mix. They are a natural extension of who I am.

It takes a while to feel at home with your gifts. They can be like a new pair of pajamas before they are washed for the first time. They feel a little stiff and uncomfortable.

Sometimes our giftedness confuses us us and we downplay our accomplishments with pronouncements of false humility. Mine reared its head in refusal of compliments.

"It was nothing."

"Anybody could do that."

"No, I'm not really any good."

Somehow that seemed to be the more spiritual response. It never occurred to me to just say, "Thank you."

Years later, I discovered that debasing our own self-worth is as much a form of self-absorption as those who can only see themselves as gifts to humanity. The truth is, both these positions are a form of self-absorption.

> *Giftedness energizes you … It draws you to activity that flows naturally.*

Giftedness energizes you. It brings you fulfillment. It draws you to activity that flows naturally. Therein lies great freedom. From this place, your intimacy with God will grow. It is his gift that enables you to know him better. As you grow in your knowledge of God, you too will increasingly understand how your unique abilities are designed for the betterment of others.

What we do for others does not seem to be the focal point of Scripture. Rather, why we do it for others seems to determine the extent to which our lives rely upon God. Our motives are the window through which God examines our soul. When self-absorption is our driving force, our achievements produce no lasting significance. (Read 1 Corinthians 13:1–8a.)

We are gifted with abilities we love to give away. The more we do so, the more fully we live and greater is the blessing we become to those around us.

Giftedness

Reflections for the Journey

How do you acknowledge your giftedness? Who can you ask to assess your gifts? How do you respond to what they say?

"O LORD, you have searched me and you know me. You know when I sit and when I rise; you perceive my thoughts from afar. You discern my going out and my lying down; you are familiar with all my ways. Before a word is on my tongue you know it completely, O LORD. You hem me in—behind and before; you have laid your hand upon me. Such knowledge is too wonderful for me, too lofty for me to attain. Where can I go from your Spirit? Where can I flee from your presence? If I go up to the heavens, you are there; if I make my bed in the depths, you are there. If I rise on the wings of the dawn, if I settle on the far side of the sea, even there your hand will guide me, your right hand will hold me fast. If I say, 'Surely the darkness will hide me and the light become night around me,' even the darkness will not be dark to you; the night will shine like the day, for darkness is as light to you. For you created my inmost being; you knit me together in my mother's womb. I praise you because I am fearfully and wonderfully made; your works are wonderful, I know that full well. My frame was not hidden from you when I was made in the secret place. When I was woven together in the depths of the earth, your eyes saw my unformed body. All the days ordained for me were written in your book before one of them came to be. How precious to me are your thoughts, O God! How vast is the sum of them! Were I to count them, they would outnumber the grains of sand. When I awake, I am still with you" (Psalm 139:1–18 NIV).

Reflections

"When I am awake, I am still with you."

Brokenness
Chapter Nine

"The first step to healing is not a step away from the pain, but a step toward it."
~ Henri Nouwen, *Life of the Beloved*

Struggle births life and passion. My life began in a war zone (Vietnam) and led me, years later, to work in refugee camps. My wife and I wrestled with isolation and loneliness. We witnessed the suffering of our own children, lost in a maddening world that swept them up without thought for their well-being. Mixed into our personal cocktail of suffering were the wounds of thousands of refugees whose pain seemed to shame me into silence. I did not dare complain when starving friends had been forced to eat corpses to survive.

How do you care for your own needs when the needs of others seem to dwarf your life?

"Broken" is one of my least favorite words. It shows up in my life in places of deep pain and confusion. It is almost always accompanied by a sense of loss and sometimes betrayal. There are some places of wounding so fresh that I fear sharing them because of the ripple effect. Some of these wounds are safely guarded secrets. If they are exposed, more people will get hurt. So brokenness carries that deep sense of loss and aloneness.

It is most deeply felt when my identity is the victim. Who am I when my foundation has been removed? What significance do I have when the definition of my life purpose seems to be taken away? What value does my life now hold?

Can you hear it? It is an old voice. It claws its way back up from the past.

> Here lies our common ground. We are all uniquely broken.

"You are ordinary. You are nobody special. You have failed again. Why did you expect this time would be different? Nobody even knows you are gone."

It is from that place you eventually discover who you really are. That is why it is a gift. From those ashes has grown a fire. It burns within you and will not be quenched. It is a call to rise. It has the familiar sound of battle. Some things are simply true. Justice is worthy of defense. Defend the broken. Hold the wounded and suffering. Cry out against the advance of systems that tear down.

Here lies our common ground. We are all uniquely broken. Our brokenness, the places where we hurt, the deep struggles and questions of our lives are part of the defining qualities that shape us. Our unique abilities and the humble wisdom that results from our times of brokenness bring clarity to our life's purpose.

Henri Nouwen's profound insights into brokenness led him to link our struggles with our strength: "When the deepest currents of our life no longer have any influence on the waves at the surface, then our vitality will eventually ebb, and we will end up listless and bored even when we are busy (Nouwen, *Life of the Beloved*)."

Our deepest currents are formed in our most painful experiences. They can leave us hard and bitter or they can birth a deep passion for the brokenness of others. I have learned to embrace the suffering that has led me to this place.

Brokenness too, is God's gift to me. Not the evil that thrived upon my ruin, but rather the flame that emerged from the ashes. He makes all things new. He changes what was intended for evil and molds it into beauty. It is our lifetime on canvas. It is a portrait of the redemption of God in your life. He invites me, he invites you to wrap your arms around our places of humbling with hearts that are thankful for all that we learned through the process. Are we finally able to consider thankfulness as a response for how he is reclaiming the scorched earth of our souls?

I have needed to plant my stake in the ground. I will not retreat from this place. I will move forward with growing clarity as the love of God breathes healing into my places of loneliness and pain, softens my heart towards the wounded and begins to move my lips to speak out against injustice. I have accepted his invitation to forgive and be forgiven.

Reflections for the Journey

What breaks your heart? Consider your deepest places of suffering. What would you not have known had you not experienced that pain?

A psalm of David:
"The Lord is my shepherd; I have everything I need. He lets me rest in green pastures. He leads me to calm water. He gives me new strength. He leads me on paths that are right for the good of his name. Even if I walk through a very dark valley, I will not be afraid, because you are with me. Your rod and your shepherd's staff comfort me. You prepare a meal for me in front of my enemies. You pour oil of blessing on my head you fill my cup to overflowing. Surely your goodness and love will be with me all my life, and I will live in the house of the Lord forever" (Psalm 23 NCV).

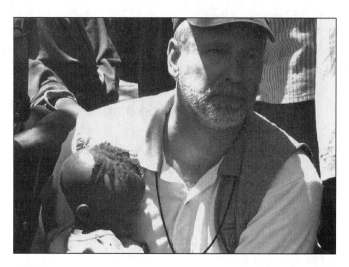

Without intervention, 8,000 babies were determined to have two weeks left of life. We managed to intervene in 2,000 lives.

Tears

Chapter Ten

Much of my callousness and invulnerability have come from my refusal to mourn the loss of a soft word and a tender embrace.
~ Brennan Manning, *Abba's Child*

I could hear the surgeon's saw as he cut off my knee joint. An amputation in that sense. I also heard the mallet driving the titanium pin into my femur. No pain, just groggy awareness that somewhere in my lower parts some major surgery was taking place. It was about a six-week process of discovery.

Laying in my hospital bed, my lower leg felt like an unfrozen ice pack; push on it and the indentations remained. My nurse ordered me to work that trapped fluid out of my leg. So diligently, I would rub and massage the gel textured liquid down towards my foot. Two days passed with a growing pain and swelling in my ankle. I asked my nurse again about it and she was shocked to hear that I was working it down towards my foot.

"It has no place to go down there. You have to work it up your leg to the lymph nodes in the groin! Otherwise you are at serious risk of blood clotting."

What do the lymph nodes do? They pass the unwanted material out of your body. Sounds logical doesn't it. If you didn't know that medical reality, the likelihood of you discovering it on your own is doubtful.

The churches of our city rented the convention centre to host worship services each night for one week. It was the beginning of the "Love Abbotsford" movement. I remember sitting in my office with a growing desire to attend. My week was full but there remained one window of opportunity, Friday night. It required a choice between retreating into the mountains for the weekend or attending the service. My conscience quipped that one was a more spiritual decision than the other. I frankly didn't care. I simply wanted to hear God and not miss the opportunity. It could have happened in either place.

I sensed I should stay. The service opened with a reading from Scripture that God had impressed upon me in a very meaningful way as a teenager. It followed with a couple of songs that had also been deeply significant. I remember thinking, "Well God, you have my attention. I know I made the right decision, so I'm listening."

Nothing jumped off the page. It ended. "So God, why did you want me to come to this?" I was actually a little disappointed.

I saw a pastor friend of mine assisting at the front of the auditorium. At least we could have a word of prayer together before I went home.

He saw me coming. I was within two feet of him when, without warning, I was literally hit with a wall of grief. I have never experienced anything like it before or since. Stumbling, I collapsed into him and he held me. I began to sob at a gut wrenching level. He just held me. My life began to flash across my thoughts like a slide show. I saw my sin played out in multiple slides. I relived many genocides; evil things that I had experienced. So much death and pain and suffering. It went on and on. I could hear people from behind, asking if I was demon possessed.

> *Without warning, I was literally hit with a wall of grief.*

I deeply appreciated his response. It was quiet and gentle and he simply said, "No, just pray. He has seen a lot."

I was struck by the simplistic thinking of people who meant well but who completely missed the point of the situation. Frankly, the experience itself was far too consuming for me to really care. I wept for over forty-five minutes, non-stop. It took me another fifteen minutes to gain some sense of composure. I will never forget my friend's words. He said, "You're not done."

I disagreed, "Oh yes I am."

He said, "No you're not."

I said to him, "I can't go through any more of this. It is too much for me."

"I'll walk with you," he said.

"I will do anything you tell me to do," I said. "Just don't ask me to make a decision on my own. I don't have any strength left."

That began one of the many journeys I have been on as God heals me on the inside while increasing my ability to know who he is and what he is like.

I have come to know and understand the purging of the filth that clutters the heart. Without a doubt, tears are God's lymph nodes of the soul. Welcome them. There are periods of time when weeping happens easily. I used to try to gain control of those moments. They are meant to be the stress relievers of the heart and often cause other people to be uncomfortable around you. We work hard to stop them, like massaging fluid down into your ankles instead of out of your body. Let them flow.

Tears have become a friend that leave me drained yet healthier. Jesus understood their power. He used the gift himself when he was at a crossroads in his own heart. In times of grief, sorrow or longing, Jesus allowed the tears to flow.

Reflections for the Journey

What is healthy sorrow? When have you wept?

"Jesus wept. Job wept. David wept. Jeremiah wept. They did it openly. Their weeping became a matter of public record... And our Savior was, as everyone knows, 'a Man of Sorrows'."
~ (Eugene Peterson) Michael Card, *A Sacred Sorrow*

Purpose
Chapter Eleven

"A good and godly man arranges within himself before-hand those things which he is outwardly to act."
~ Thomas à Kempis, *Imitations of Christ*

Why am I surprised when God answers my questions? He was persistent. It took several years for his voice to penetrate my understanding. When it did, it simply said, *"I am not dependent upon you."*

That couldn't be true. My whole life revolved around voices of guilt. "God ain't gonna be happy if you don't produce. His Kingdom can't advance if you don't pull your weight."

"I don't need you."

Yes, you do God! I'm necessary. Otherwise, why have I beat myself up all these years? What is my purpose in life?

Purpose has something to do with leaving a mark, right? A large enough impression that people will say I lived well?

Maybe that is the wrong question. Yet significance is a deep-seated longing, even if it is different than purpose. Purpose seems to focus on the "why" of life and significance on the quality and effect. They coexist, but I can only understand life's significance when I understand my purpose. And my purpose is only understood when I know the one who created me.

The pot doesn't say to the Potter, "I want to be elegant, or useful, or contemporary." The pot simply fulfills what it was designed to do.

For many years I struggled to find that design in my life. Lists of appropriate behavior had to be considered and others' expectations factored in. What would they think, or worse, what would they say? At the end of the day, I was only living the sentiments of others.

"Why" questions find fertile ground in me. I can't let them go easily because they take me deeper than template answers.

> *The pot simply fulfills what it was designed to do.*

Why God? Why did you create me?

Initially I thought his answer was, "Because I need you to do my work. People need you to help them." So I plunged into serving God with a genuine fervor, but the goal lines kept moving. It was never enough because there was always more to do. Was I really committed? Was I doing God's will or my will? How was I to know the difference?

Looking back, I can see specific gifts in my life from God. Mix those together with my times of brokenness and I emerge a unique personality that finds common ground with everyone I meet.

God has granted me great freedom. It rests on a foundation of worship. I have discovered that what I choose to worship will reveal the purpose of my life. As long as my worship is directed towards my Creator, it is difficult to stray far from things that please him. When my worship moves inward, to a selfish place, then I am at risk.

Purpose doesn't just happen. It is intentional. It is refined as we develop our ability to listen, especially to the quiet voice of God and the counsel of others. Although the prophet Jeremiah penned these words for the people of Israel thousands of years ago, they remain relevant for you and me today: *"For I know the plans I have for you,' says the Lord. 'They are plans for good and not for disaster, to give you a future and a hope'"* (Jeremiah 29:11).

I used to think God would send me to the exact place that I did not want to go. In reality, he did, but for different reasons than I originally understood.

My childish impressions were of a God who had a sadistic twist. He would search my heart for the things I hated and coerce me. He was the parent who made his children eat spinach and onions and garlic while the cookies and ice cream remained just out of reach. If God's will didn't include some level of sacrifice and suffering, I thought the spiritual effect would somehow be less significant.

It is a stark contrast to living fully and abundantly.

I have discovered God does allow suffering into my life. He does place the onions and spinach on my plate. Not as a substitute for ice cream; more a prerequisite to eating in an ice cream parlor, with an unlimited tab.

People can do unspeakable things. People are not God. We want him to intervene, just not in our lives. We expect him to stop others without restricting our freedom.

God operates not with a dictatorial bent but rather from his desire to protect me (often from myself). It might be fear. It might be laziness. It might be selfish self-absorption. Whatever my reasons for resisting God in my life, I realize now that we are known by him and he has created us with unique tendencies that he desires to refine. Trusting him with that opens the adventure.

Reflections for the Journey

How has your uniqueness—your gifts as well as your brokenness—served in creating a purpose that you are passionate about?

Purpose

Trust in the Lord with all your heart, and lean not on your own understanding. In all your ways, acknowledge him, and he will make your paths straight (Proverbs 3:5–6 NIV).

———••••———

"For I know the plans I have for you," declares the Lord, plans to prosper you and not to harm you, plans to give you hope and a future (Jeremiah 29:11 NIV).

———••••———

"What comes into our minds when we think about God is the most important thing about us."
~ A. W. Tozer, *Knowledge of the Holy*

———••••———

"If God be your partner, make your plans large."
~ D. L. Moody

Humility

Chapter Twelve

Humility is the ability to enjoy the value of others.

Have you ever wondered where you ranked on the humility scale? It's a slippery slope isn't it? Once you begin to think that you are humble, you cease to be humble. Everyone loves a humble person. No one loves a person who thinks they are humble. How is one to know if they are succeeding in humility? Possibly with the realization that humility has nothing to do with us.

Easy to love, with much love to give.

In the late 90's, former Soviet Satellite States had no structure to support children with physical or mental disabilities. Most were euthanized or kept hidden in the family home. Building and operating a school based on the L'Arche Community model, enabled us to watch public attitudes soften towards these children. It was the first school for children with disabilities in Uzbekistan, and to my knowledge, the first in all the "Stans".

Humility is the ability to enjoy the value of others. It flows from a generous spirit and finds true pleasure in seeing others succeed. There is a selflessness to humility that cannot be fabricated. We either genuinely love others or we are individuals who tend to love ourselves first, then others according to their level of deserved favor.

Watch the parents of a newborn. They tend to be lost in the love of their child. They become children themselves as they coo and gawk and reduce themselves to ridiculous forms. They

> *Humility finds true pleasure in seeing others succeed.*

are oblivious to the opinions of others and are enraptured by the innocence of a tiny child whose life is laid in their hands. Likewise, the child responds with unconditional trust.

Jesus said that unless we become as little children, we will never be able to enter the Kingdom of God. I think he meant that without innocence and trust, we just won't "get it;" like listening to a foreign language. Sadly, some limit Jesus' words to mean, "I won't get into heaven."

In reality, Jesus understood that unless we come to the place of true humility and generosity, we will stifle our living. Our ability to live fully and freely will be hampered by our own inclination to put our interests first. We then limit our pursuit to sources of fulfillment he knows we will enjoy.

From that perspective, it is difficult to recognize joy-filled opportunities in the happiness of others. Selfishness significantly limits our ability to be blessed. It is a great irony because most pursue selfish intentions in their quest for greater pleasure.

Humility? Become a child who delights in the freedom that exists before suspicion; who embraces the freedom that chooses to trust rather than doubt; who desires to see others live well as much as you desire to live well yourself.

Reflections for the Journey

"Jesus called a little child to him and put the child among them. Then he said, 'I tell you the truth, unless

you turn from your sins and become like little children, you will never get into the Kingdom of Heaven. So anyone who becomes as humble as this little child is the greatest in the Kingdom of Heaven' " (Matthew 18:2–4).

———

"So humble yourselves under the mighty power of God, and at the right time he will lift you up in honor. Give all your worries and cares to God, for he cares about you" (1 Peter 5:6–7).

Consider your top five sources of joy and fulfillment. Where would you place them on the following scale?

for others   1   2   3   4   5   6   7   8   9   for self

$\longleftrightarrow$

"They rather choose to be great than humble, therefore they become vain in their imaginations. He is truly great that is great in charity. He is truly great that is little in himself, and that maketh no account of any height of honor."
     ~ Thomas à Kempis, *Imitation of Christ*

———

"In the same way, you younger men must accept the authority of the elders. And all of you, serve each other in humility, for 'God opposes the proud but favors the humble' " (1 Peter 5:5).

Charity
Chapter Thirteen

"Let my heart be broken with the things that break the heart of God."
~ Bob Pierce

I walked with a colleague who, while in Uganda, had miraculously escaped execution by Idi Amin. We were in what remained of the botanical gardens of Kampala — such carnage.

I have also been with child soldiers in the North, who escaped years of forced bondage, rape and murder—such evil.

Through these experiences I have come to understand some of the concepts written by another man who survived Amin's genocide.

In *A Distant Grief*, Kefa Sempangi writes, "(I learned) that unless I was broken, I would be too proud to lose my life for a sinner. I would be too proud to give my life away for people who were not perfect. I would wait for the perfect person and the perfect community, and I would never find them. I would end up like Judas, making only a partial commitment to the body of believers to whom I belonged. Yet my identity would be found in my own independence from that same group and rebellion from those same people."

Working for an international aid agency, I found myself repeatedly in circumstances of heartbreaking need. Weekly, pleas for help would cross my desk. We simply did not have the capacity to respond. Most times my answer had to be "No". I lived with the realization that people died as a result of my decision. The burden became overwhelming. In its own twisted way, it became a point of self-pity. Unconsciously, I was choosing between people's perceptions of a life of exemplary sacrifice and the reality that God had not asked me to be a savior. Personal grandeur is difficult to resist.

The penetrating questions I ask myself expose the gap between service for my own sake and service submitted to God's intentions. Read Scripture and it becomes obvious that God's sovereignty does not require assistance.

God is God. He is dependent on no other to complete himself or his work. He must therefore have another reason for inviting our participation. I am slowly learning that his invitation to serve clarifies the value of the small, the simple, the pure and true. It creates fertile ground in my soul, allowing God's transformation to begin in me. He longs for me to serve others to buffer me from my own self-ishness. He desires service for my benefit. The world only needs one Savior.

Too often our charity is delivered as "aid." It seeks to repair what is broken in others yet fails to see what is broken in ourselves. Whether that is our intention, aid often creates an atmosphere of expectation and entitlement. Unless it is offered with great discretion, aid allows people to quit believing in themselves. It undermines initiative and weakens the human sprit.

> *Our charity seeks to repair what is broken in others yet fails to see what is broken in ourselves.*

President Kagami of Rwanda challenged his people. "There is no dignity or self-esteem," he said, "in being fed by other taxpayers' monies. It is demeaning (Kivu Retreat Speech, 2009)."

A good father longs to support and encourage his children. He takes great pride in their advances towards generous living. He invests in their development each time he provides opportunities to experience the joy of caring for others. When a father shares those experiences with his child, their love and appreciation of each other deepens. Therein lies the link between a Heavenly Father's love and the underlying motive for service.

Although he is not dependent on me, Jesus invites me to serve. He invites me to focus on those other than myself.

When we respond to the needs of others, it softens our arrogance. We become fertile ground for the Spirit of God to cultivate seeds that Scripture describes as fruit of the Spirit: love, joy, peace, patience, kindness, goodness, faithfulness, gentleness and self-control. (Read Galatians 5:22–23.) Sometimes it is worthwhile to pause and reflect upon profound truth.

Each invitation extended by the Spirit of God to invest in the life of another breathes life into our places of brokenness. We are all in need of the healing. The deepest pain is only remedied through the posture of serving others.

Reflections for the Journey

When you see a person sleeping on a sidewalk, does their condition reveal anything to you about your own area of need? Is our personal brokenness revealed more clearly by that person's condition?

> *"How different would our life be if we could but believe that every little act of faithfulness, every gesture of love, every word of forgiveness, every little bit of joy and peace will multiply and multiply as long as there are people to receive it."*
> ~ Henri Nouwen, *Life of the Beloved*

> *"...Free those who are wrongly imprisoned; lighten the burden of those who work for you. Let the oppressed go free, and remove the chains that bind people. Share your food with the hungry, and give shelter to the homeless. Give clothes to those who need them, and do not hide from relatives who need your help. Then your salvation will come like the dawn, and your wounds will quickly heal. Your godliness will lead you forward, and the glory of the Lord will protect you from behind. Then when you call, the Lord will answer. 'Yes, I am here,' he will quickly reply"* (Isaiah 58:6–9).

Service
Chapter Fourteen

We may need the poor more than the poor need us.

It is interesting to see how childhood Bible stories influence one's perspective on life. The story of the Good Samaritan, for example, has appreciably shaped my attitude towards the needy. The story of Jesus' instructions to a rich young man—"Sell all you have, give it to the poor and come follow me."—influenced my opinion about wealth and stewardship. Somewhere, tucked away in my psyche, grew an embryonic attitude towards wealth, sacrifice and spiritual service.

Ironic, that after thirty years of studying the Bible and teaching, I realized that both those stories begin with an identical question asked by two different men. The answers Jesus gave were remarkably different. Why?

It was not Christ's intent to establish a theological treatise on wealth, sacrifice, service or holiness. Jesus answer simply moved past the symptomatic question to a root issue that rested in the heart of each of these men. That root still lives.

The question asked was, "What do I have to do to inherit eternal life?"

Jesus refocused it, exposing the limited extent of their love for God and others.

It is no surprise to hear that God deserves all of my heart. Add to that, all of my soul, and my strength and my mind. I can go through an entire day without ever considering it. I can commit myself to worship and study while allowing anger towards another to fester in my soul.

Jesus thrusts the question into the open. If I do not love my neighbor as much as I love myself, who do I love more? If I love myself more than my neighbor, do I have the ability to love God with all of my heart?

My perspective of myself colors all I see in others. The realization that God simply loves me without conditions sets me free from striving. It allows room in my priorities to be a blessing to others for their sake; not a quota requirement or an incremental hike on a holiness meter.

I need my neighbors. They become someone to focus upon other than myself. Each of them would treasure being blessed. Therein is the magic, or maybe more appropriately—the wonder.

God longs for us to serve because it is in that position of humility that he works our transformation. Any time we invest in something other than ourselves, we take a submissive posture. From this place of submission, God begins our metamorphosis into his image.

It is a sobering moment to realize that, from God's perspective, the ultimate reason for our acts of service is for our benefit. In this context we begin to realize how much we are in need of relationship with others. Those in need provide the perfect opportunity for us to serve. They come to us in all shapes and sizes, from every economic level and position. When we serve, we release the attitudes of entitlement, the demands for our rights and the temptation to allow pleasure to dominate responsibility.

> *God longs for us to serve because it is in that position of humility that he works our transformation.*

In that respect, we may need the poor more than the poor need us. This realization helped me recognize my "Big Brother" posture. People do not want us to fix their problems for them. They want to be valued and have their God-given dignity restored. They desire to be enabled to meet their own needs.

Reflections for the Journey

Remember a time when helping someone else brought deep significance to your own life. How are you different today because of the generosity you have either received or exhibited?

———•———

"...Remove the heavy yoke of oppression. Stop pointing your finger and spreading vicious rumors! Feed the hungry, and help those in trouble. Then your light will shine out from the darkness, and the darkness around you will be as bright as noon. The Lord will guide you continually, giving you water when you are dry and restoring your strength. You will be like a well-watered garden, like an ever-flowing spring" (Isaiah 58:9b–11).

Transformation
Chapter Fifteen

"A humble knowledge of thyself is a surer way to God than a deep search after learning."
~ Thomas à Kempis, Imitation of Christ

As a young college student, I attended a lecture I might otherwise have forgotten except for a statement Keith Price made that drew my pen from my pocket and recorded itself on a scrap of paper. I knew it was true the moment I heard it. I knew that if… if I followed its advice, this statement would lead me to places my heart longed for. It was a turning point in my life. That transformation is continuing and the statement still rings true in my soul.

"You will become like what you expose yourself to. The more you gaze upon God, the more you will become like him."

Was it possible to become more like God in behavior and attitude simply by being exposed to him? I had constantly lost the fight of trying to be good enough. It resulted in begging God for forgiveness, only to fail again. I would continually come to the place of not wanting to even ask God for help because I wasn't convinced I honestly wanted it. If I couldn't convince myself, did I have any hope that God would believe that I was sincere?

Guilt and the shame from continual confession were the predominant voices in my mind. I assumed my failures alienated me; a holy "time out" in the corner for David. They told me God didn't want me in his room.

So I would rehearse the procedure. Knowing I had already managed to sin, repent and sin again within a six-hour period, it seemed logical that I couldn't possibly repent again because God wouldn't believe me. By waiting until tomorrow, my personal disgust with myself would have subsided. Maybe then I could repent again and really mean it. I never sensed he was surprised; just disappointed.

> *You will become like what you expose yourself to.*

Keith Price's statement shifted my focus. It took me to a place of questioning my excuses. Had I been approaching this inner battle in a completely wrong way?

God's Spirit summarized the transformation in my soul this way:

"Quit trying to quit. You spend so much energy there and you still fail. In fact, you spend so much effort that it encompasses your thinking, your dreams, your waking moments. It's no wonder you can't break free. It consumes your life! Quit! Replace effort with an increased desire to simply get to know me. Find out what I am like. Expose yourself to me and I will begin my work in you. Right now you may not want to walk this road with me because so many other things are attractive, appealing, alluring. You don't want to say, 'I leave these things behind.' That's fine. Don't say it.

"If you want, I will give you the desire to desire me. As that desire grows, it will become part of you. The things that held you before will lose their power over you and I will set you free.

"Quit. Let me. My yoke is easy. My burden is light. I came that you might have life and have it abundantly. I have come to set the captive free. I am the source, the way, the truth and the life. Take advantage of it.

"Quit, and gaze upon me."

In an emergency, a traumatized person often does not know where to turn. Panicked, they need the voice of their rescuer to call out their name and focus their attention.

"David. Look at me. Look at me!" And when we do, we can begin to follow instructions that will bring us out of the carnage.

God is an inviting God.

"Look at me! Abide in me and I will abide in you. Live and find your life in the Vine and I will produce the fruit. Come and become like me. Your transformation is not up to you." (Read John 15.)

Transformation

Reflections for the Journey

Have you ever tried to break a habit and failed? Are you open to the idea of re-channeling your efforts? Rather than focusing on an addiction, consider spending the same amount of time and energy with the person of Jesus; reading his words, experiencing his creation and meeting with others who have journeyed with him? The challenge is to see whether exposure to Christ changes your desires and reduces the power that addictions once held over you.

———•••——

"For God is working in you, giving you the desire and the power to do what pleases him" (Philippians 2:13).

67

Voices

Chapter Sixteen

"Look! I stand at the door and knock. If you hear my voice and open the door, I will come in, and we will share a meal together as friends" (Revelations 3:20).

What if we never asked the question, "What if…?"

Nancy (my wife) and I are entering a new stage in our relationship with each other and with God. We have both been taught and told many things about God throughout our lives. We have experienced some very unique circumstances from which we formed opinions about God. Somewhere in our journey we picked up the concept that sacrifice was more honoring to God than blessing. Sorrow was a stronger indicator of spirituality than joy. If there was no suffering, our commitment wasn't deep enough. Think about those statements. Are they accurate?

Each statement is a grid to process life's experiences.

At different times in my life, I defined my significance experientially. If I had a girlfriend I was more significant than if I didn't. Having a good paying job was more noteworthy than struggling to survive. Being a CEO was worthy of attention. Being the founder of something signaled success. Voices, all telling me whether I was measuring up. Yet why do they wield such influence? Power, position and wealth do attract a certain following who quickly abandon you if none of those three positions remain.

A second reality stems from within. If a colleague is honored for an achievement you both had accomplished and you were overlooked, would you celebrate their success or struggle with resentment and envy? When your friend discovers that his investments have far exceeded his expectations, is there an irritation with his success, knowing that you had not received the advice from which he benefited?

Inner voices constantly compare and make assumptions. "Beware of life. It will turn you more dirty deals than profitable ones."

The enticement of each voice is the subtle promise of a place of recognition. It is the home I've always wanted; the community where I am accepted; the place of influence where I have a sense of belonging. They tempt us in our places of vulnerability.

In spite of the many enticing counterfeits, we have only one true home. It is the place where God is. It is our place beside our Father who continually speaks value into our lives. Some have fathers who have done the opposite, resulting in voices that tell them fathers can't be trusted. They are lured away by another promise of a safer place; a community that will care for them. Yet the foundations of every counterfeit assurance are eventually exposed. There is a quiet voice however that leads us back to our true home. It is the one place that we all have been created for.

> *Voices are given power when we believe what they say.*

Voices are given power when we believe what they say, and do what they demand. When we recognize that there is only one voice that truly has our best interests at heart; that knows what we were created for; that has established home for us—only then will the other voices lose their influence and control over us.

Jesus repeatedly said, "He who has ears to hear, let him hear."

Reflections for the Journey

Which voices have power or influence over you? If this is a topic of importance to you, consider reading Henri Nouwen's book, *The Return of the Prodigal Son*.

Reflections

"The gatekeeper opens the gate for him, and the sheep recognize his voice and come to him. He calls his own sheep by name and leads them out. After he has gathered his own flock, he walks ahead of them, and they follow him because they know his voice. They won't follow a stranger; they will run from him because they don't know his voice. I am the good shepherd; I know my own sheep, and they know me, just as my Father knows me and I know the Father. So I sacrifice my life for the sheep. I have other sheep, too, that are not in this sheepfold. I must bring them also. They will listen to my voice, and there will be one flock with one shepherd" (John 10:3–5, 14–16).

Truth
Chapter Seventeen

"...You are truly my disciples if you remain faithful to my teachings. And you will know the truth, and the truth will set you free" (John 8:31b–32).

Some principles transcend time. They were true millions of years ago, they are true today and will remain so. Yet how do I know that circumstance cannot alter truth?

Tongues stick to metal in -30F weather. That is an eternal truth. Anyone who has lived in temperatures of -30F has been compelled, in spite of 100 warnings to the contrary, to touch their tongue to a piece of metal. Once adhered, they cannot control the desperate urge to pull free, even if it costs them a piece of flesh on metal. Truth doesn't change.

We all believe something. Choosing to believe something doesn't make it true. Whether we admit it or not, it requires faith. Those beliefs shape each of us. Even atheists require an element of faith to believe there is no God. Eventually everyone acknowledges the reality that some things are inherently true and will remain so. These are more than a concept. They are foundational with Truth as the Source, not a byproduct. The fact that God loves me only crystallized after years of life experience, including circumstances that seemed to contradict that fact.

Periodically we stumble with the discovery that a deep conviction is proven to be wrong. On those occasions we walk through dark times. Our lives flounder for awhile, seeking someone to blame, anyone, for the wasted years of our investment in a lie.

> *Choosing to believe something doesn't make it true.*

Times of reflection bring clarity on those points. The more people delve into knowing truth, the closer they are drawn to its source. That journey has two paths, or perhaps represents two sides of a coin: the pursuit of truth (things true) and the pursuit of Truth (the source and definition). Both disciplines introduce God to us in new ways.

Jeremiah said it best. *"You will seek me and find me when you seek me with all your heart"* (Jeremiah 29:13 NIV). Jesus clarified it by stating, *"I am the way, the truth and the life. No one comes to the Father except through me"* (John 14:6 NIV).

Few people take the time to reflect upon what they honestly believe. So we find ourselves embarrassed by what seems to be a contradiction in our behavior. We are tempted to make excuses rather than face the reality that something within our beliefs gave us permission to do what we have done. It is a worthwhile exercise to discover those convictions and bring them forward into our conscious decision making.

It isn't an easy process, but it is a revealing one. We will discover lies that have defined us, even from childhood. They influence our opinions.

Knowing what we believe and understanding what we value brings greater consistency in our actions. The baggage in our lives can become a gift if it causes us to better understand who we really are and recognize our potential when we surrender the load to Christ. All of us who seek meaning in life also seek to close the gap between what we say we believe and how we live each day.

There is something captivating about truth. When you hear it, when you experience it, it confirms with your spirit that it is true.

Jesus' invitation is to come to Truth and Truth will set you free.

Reflections for the Journey

How does your behavior reveal what you value? If you sensed the need to have greater harmony between what you believe and your behavior, which would need to be adjusted?

What would be required for you to not fear the revelation of your deepest secrets?

Globalization
Chapter Eighteen

"The fragmentation and commercialization of our milieu makes it nearly impossible to find a place where our whole being—body, mind, and heart—can feel safe and protected."
~ Henri Nouwen, *Life of the Beloved*

Have you ever felt like a very small fish in the ocean? The feeling of insignificance is reality for many people.

"Does anybody know I exist? Does anybody really care. What can one person do?" These questions, if not dealt with, do not diminish with time.

Pay It Forward is the story of a young boy who thought of doing one kind act for four different people and they individually had to pay that act of kindness forward to four more people. The perfect pyramid scheme to shape a culture.

Before the mid 1990s, it was virtually impossible for one person to influence change on a global scale. That is no longer true today. An article posted on a website can be read anywhere in the world. Electronic communication becomes more sophisticated every three months (probably sooner).

I have mastered the art of crashing the most uncrashable computers available to humanity. As a result, there is a 1-800 number at my disposal, with a technician who has a slight accent. That usually baits my curiosity and I will eventually ask, "Where in the world are you right now?" Over 50 percent of the time, that person is in a call station in India or Bangladesh. Amazing. They have been trained to respond to my questions with great patience. They are briefed on my cultural norms and coached on how to address my queries. They will find the solution for me.

They are the night shift, coming in at 1 a.m. to accommodate my call at 2 p.m. in Vancouver, British Columbia, Canada.

The world was brought into the living rooms of every North American on September 11, 2001. Yet few understood that we already had opened our homes to the world. The spread of globalization is the byproduct of a demand for inexpensive labor that cannot be replicated in North America.

The book, *The World is Flat*, describes the weakening of multinationals as individuals gain the ability to speak to the world from any home, hut or shanty town. Technology has been out-sourced to the point that we receive technical assistance from Bangalore, India, when we are having difficulties with our telephones or computer software. Globalization helps us understand that we do not live in isolation from the rest of the world.

That recognition is the starting place for global responsibility. Understand that God's invitation is for the restoration of all things. His covenant with Abraham was to be a father of many nations. Yet the starting point for global thinking is the second chapter of Genesis. We are the stewards of creation.

> *Globalization is too vast to not include God.*

God is the God of the nations. Many have not understood the implications of his sovereignty beyond Jesus' final command. Even that has often been reduced to, "Go into all the world and get as many people saved as you can." Yet, it is a call to disciple whole nations or people groups, to have an impact on systems and structures and to influence the shapers of culture.

With multiculturalism gaining influence, we need to recognize a biblical culture that transcends culture. We honor God as we honor what he has made. It is good to be reminded that our responsibility for life around us is not restricted by time, space and position.

Reflections

No shoes. Not a pair. Not in winter or summer. Life requires resilience in Afghanistan. Life is less complex in North America.

For those who are weary of the magnitude of the bombardment on our senses; for those who feel they cannot add one more thing to pressures caused by globalization; for those who believe that faith and globalization do not belong in the same discussion, recognize this:

Globalization is too vast to not include God. It is not simply multi-nationals penetrating global markets. It is also the creation of a global market. It is a redefining of our world to accommodate greater integration of cultures and economies on a global scale. Without God's guiding principles, we cannot maneuver the maze of decisions that affect thousands with whom we will have no physical contact.

Reflections for the Journey

Who is your neighbor? Are global issues your issues? Do you think that your decisions could influence the living conditions of people on the other side of the world? (Read Luke 10:25–37.)

Worldview
Chapter Nineteen

*Just because I say I believe something,
doesn't mean that I actually do.*

What do I honestly believe? It is easy to confuse knowledge with conviction. I've thought I've believed many things but when push came to shove, I realized that not everything I know is worth fighting for. Knowledge is not the same as conviction. Knowledge is sterile, whereas conviction and belief are living and active and guide the decisions of your heart.

Grace is one truth I have come to love. Imagine what we would deserve if we were judged according to every thought, every word and every action we have ever committed. Who could declare they were innocent? I love the idea of grace.

Ironically, I also deeply value justice. When someone wrongs me, I want justice.

"Vindicate me God. Protect me. Declare my innocence in front of those who now question my integrity."

I laughed at David (King of Israel) when, in his whining, he penned, "Lord, have mercy on me. Make me well again, so I can pay them back! (friends who had betrayed him)" (Ps. 41:10).

Strange how concepts like grace can evaporate so quickly in the face of our own sense of entitlement.

Do I honestly want to live under the power of grace, or just grace for me? Do I desire all of God's truth or only portions of it; the ones that can be spun for my benefit?

How often do you journey to deeply personal places?

"Whom should I marry?"

"What do I want to do with my life?"

"Why does evil happen to good people?"

"Why do evil people seem to get away with such cruel acts?"

"Shouldn't I have a purpose that guides my life?"

"How do I define significance?"

I've asked God each of these questions and many more. I'm not looking for easy answers. The fact that life is complex, with some answers lost in the struggle, increases the challenge to pursue it. Why settle for hollow solutions? If that is the final outcome, it would appear I simply created my own set of absolutes and my own god, who becomes easy to explain and define.

God is far more complex. Come to places where there are no answers. Live in the question for awhile rather than strive to have it resolved. Be willing to journey with God rather than simply take a trip.

Your worldview provides your limits for discovery. It is the boundary and the principles that enable you to make informed decisions. It won't necessarily demand only one response at each turn in the road, but it will provide you with common sense and discernment that can protect you from walking off a cliff on a foggy morning.

Worldview has also been compared to the glasses you wear. You see all of life through those lenses. If you have never enjoyed progressive lenses, you may not be able to appreciate the fact that they distort reality to a degree. Yet they enable you to see far more clearly than if you were not wearing them. I didn't realize however, that they also make straight lines appear slightly concave.

> *When Jesus asked, "Do you want to be well?" he was asking, "Do you want to be whole?"*

The second day of wearing my progressive lenses found me on a platform about four feet off the ground. I was preaching in Edmonton. Pulpits are restrictive to me and I am known to wander as I interact with the audience. On that particular morning, I walked to the edge of the concave platform, only to discover that it wasn't concave. I landed half on, half off the communion table on my way to the floor. Looking up from my prone position, I saw a young man with his video camera. Climbing back on stage, I attempted to regain the attention of the audience, but it wasn't meant to be.

Worldview will either give you clarity of sight on life's edges, or it will distort and twist your vision. It is important to know what you believe.

Reflections for the Journey

Read the following sentences. Do they ring true or false? Why or why not?

"All roads lead to heaven."

"If people work hard, they can succeed."

"I earned what I own and I deserve it."

"People of like kind should stay together."

Is there a consistent theme to your responses?

"But watch out! Be careful never to forget what you yourself have seen. Do not let these memories escape from your mind as long as you live! And be sure to pass them on to your children and grandchildren. Never forget the day when you stood before the Lord your God at Mount Sinai..." (Deuteronomy 4:9–10a).

Trust
Chapter Twenty

"I will praise your mighty deeds, O Sovereign Lord. I will tell everyone that you alone are just" (Psalm 71:16).

One day, I am going to have to write a book entitled, *I Almost Lost My Faith When It Rained On My Drywall.* You would think that a simple thing like rain on drywall board would not shake a person's faith, especially when that person had had experiences significantly more traumatic. I have lived in genocides, seen humanity at our worst, witnessed indescribable cruelty and still emerged with a deep conviction that God is loving, sovereign, trustworthy and just. But the rain on my drywall blindsided me, leaving me off guard and vulnerable.

I checked the Doppler forecast. No rain for three days. Not a cloud on the horizon. If ever there was a time to change the vinyl deck covering, it was now. My son-in-law managed everything for me. Having removed the old vinyl, we quickly discovered that the deck was infested with carpenter ants. One entire corner had no support holding it in place apart from the metal frame of the garage door. Not convenient, but not insurmountable. Stuff happens. It would be okay, there was no rain in sight.

They stripped the plywood off the deck, cut out the infested wood, brought in the exterminator and began re-building everything by the end of the first day. We could have this project finished by tomorrow.

In the middle of the night, I heard the rain. Tarps proved not to be water proof. I laid them over the exposed beams of what had been my front deck. Soon the water was pooling between the rafters. I spent much of the night dumping water as it pooled but that didn't prevent it from running through onto the internal drywall of the roof in my garage. In that garage lay the collected mass possessions of our oldest two children.

Sitting on rafters for most of the night leaves a person with much time to talk with God. It wasn't that amiable.

"You did this. It has to be you because Doppler said there wasn't a cloud in the sky. All clear. No rain for three days. This is you."

It was the beginning of a struggle about what I honestly believe.

It is easy to say that God is sovereign. The Bible teaches that. He can do whatever he wants, when he wants, for whatever reason he wants. That's sovereignty. He made it all and stays completely engaged. I was acknowledging that, but it wasn't comforting. Why?

> *If he can't be trusted, do I want to surrender to him? Is he protecting my back?*

Because I was beginning to realize that I questioned whether he was good. Could I trust that he had my best interest at heart? How does rain on my drywall benefit me? What was he thinking?

So the issue I began to question was not his sovereignty. It was his goodness and his justice. If he can't be trusted, do I want to surrender to him? Is he protecting my back? The "trip" mentality tells you to "just believe." The journey gives you freedom to live in the questions for awhile and discover things about God that you will never learn in a classroom.

Reflections for the Journey

Where do you place your trust? Do you question God? When the trustworthiness of God is questioned, where do you turn?

"Our God is a God who saves! The Sovereign Lord rescues us from death" (Psalm 68:20).

Reflections

"Don't let those who trust in you be ashamed because of me, O Sovereign Lord of Heaven's Armies. Don't let me cause them to be humiliated, O God of Israel" (Psalm 69:6).

"But as for me, how good it is to be near God! I have made the Sovereign Lord my shelter, and I will tell everyone about the wonderful things you do" (Psalm 73:28).

"But deal well with me, O Sovereign Lord, for the sake of your own reputation! Rescue me because you are so faithful and good" (Psalm 109:21).

"O Sovereign Lord, the strong one who rescued me, you protected me on the day of battle" (Psalm 140:7).

"I look to you for help, O Sovereign Lord. You are my refuge; don't let them kill me" (Psalm 141:8).

Trust

Trust.

Guilt
Chapter Twenty-one

False Guilt is a wonderful tool in the handbag of motivation.

My own questions, when left unanswered, opened the door to further doubt. What if God exists but he can't prevent things? What if he's out there but isn't able to protect us? What if that rain on my drywall was not the result of his doing but rather an example of his inability to prevent it?

Suddenly, my foundation was not nearly as stable. Try as I might, I could not stop the spiraling, until I stopped looking for the answer.

I was afraid of my own doubt. My questions, when hurled, seemed to be no more penetrating than the pounding of an infant's hand on a stone wall. What I didn't realize was that those same questions drove me to dig deeper and discover the source of my doubts. They became the places of wonderful discovery.

Even though these questions have all been asked before, it does not mean that you are not allowed to ask them again. Our questions are meant to become our friends. They can be a safe place for us to vent, wrestle, wonder, search and discover.

Some have concluded that God simply cannot or will not help them. He has set the stage, laid the ground rules and now expects us to live by them. He may want to intervene, but is unable to. As a result, if God's will on earth is going to get done, we have to do it. (Study Deism.)

Guilt

That may sound blasphemous to some but you may have worn this set of lenses in your lifetime. This worldview requires us to step in to help God out. When people think this way, what is the primary conviction?

"God needs me. If I don't do his will, it won't get done."

"People's eternity is in your hands."

"You are the only one left. No one else will do this. You have to do this."

It is all the same lie. The primary motivator is guilt.

I hated when guilt was used to try to force me to perform. It held an incredible power over me for years and stored up in my heart an overflowing of resentment.

Guilt is a wonderful tool in the handbag of motivation. It's also one we've all probably used once or twice ourselves.

Many times my church would tell me that God needed my help for his will to be done. He was relying upon us (me) to get the job done. And it became one more opportunity for me to fail.

What kind of God hasn't the power to accomplish his will? Why would I come to view God through that set of lenses? What would cause me to place more confidence in myself than in the God I was supposed to serve? To be honest, if you examine the true motives

> *Many times my church would tell me that God needed my help for his will to be done.*

behind this conviction you discover an over-inflated ego and a good dose of arrogance. Whoever sits in this place of power will be tempted to exploit others with it.

"God needs you to get his will done?"

It is easy to be misunderstood on this point. The Bible's invitation is to act. Care for the needy, the widow, the sick, the marginalized, the weak. Speak out against injustice. Yet the combination of all these commands does not lead us to the conclusion that God is unable to do these things without people. God is sovereign and he can do whatever he wishes to do. The invitation to serve must be motivated by something other than his inability to accomplish his work on earth.

Reflections

We were made to have communion with God. He is leading you there. Rather than needing your help, his invitation is to release yourself from the burden of propping up God's kingdom for him. Spend your energy exposing yourself to him in every situation. Allow your response to others to flow from a heart's longing to honor and serve God.

Reflections for the Journey

Does the place you find yourself seem overwhelming? What weight are you carrying that belongs to God?

Do you ever use guilt as a tool of persuasion? When tempted to use it again, consider whether you have the other person's best interest at heart.

He lives with the question why he is the only survivor in 20,000. Why did the bullet in his head not save him from having the questions with no answers?

Himself

"Once it was the blessing, now it is the Lord;
Once t'was painful trying, now 'tis perfect trust.
Once 'twas busy planning, now 'tis trustful prayer
Once 'twas anxious caring, now He has the care;
Once I tried to use Him, now He uses me;"
~ A. B. Simpson

Programs
Chapter Twenty-two

"As long as you live in the world, yielding to its enormous pressures to prove to yourself and to others that you are somebody, and knowing from the beginning that you will lose in the end, your life can be scarcely more than a long struggle for survival."
~ Henri Nouwen, *Life of the Beloved*

I live in a community known as the "Gun Belt". It has been known in the past as the "Bible Belt". When citizens begin to ask how this slide into violence came to be, I am mystified at their inability to figure it out. If God is not an influence in our decision making, then who determines what is right and what is wrong? If God in reality does not exist, if he is just a narcotic for the weak minded, then who is to say that violence is inappropriate for our culture? It is a subjective foundation.

Many have been exposed to those who believe in God but expect nothing from him. They look at the deists and wonder why they need God at all. If God can't help me, then it is a fairly weak argument to try to defend him. If I end up having to defend God, then the chances are I am the one telling you what God is like; what he can and cannot do. In fact, in the process of making those declarations, I have simply replaced God with myself.

The gods we create tickle and tease. They supply us with pleasure and entertain. We are constantly told that we deserve better. Strive for what we can't afford. Credit is a blessing not a curse.

The church is not immune to the same temptations. When confronted with shrinking numbers in a congregation, churches often resort to improving programs without consulting God. Success is then measured by program statistics rather than the transforma-

> *We are told we deserve better. Strive for what we can't afford. Credit is a blessing not a curse.*

tional work of God. It becomes no different than non-religious activity.

People behave the way they do primarily because of beliefs, not because of programs. If we tackle the issues without challenging the thinking, we haven't moved one step closer to sustainable change.

In today's secular world, culture's morals and values are formed by one of three sources: those with the loudest voice, those with the most voices, or those with the most power. In every scenario that fails to recognize God as real, all-powerful, loving and just, people will rise up and attempt to establish their own norms and laws for society.

Have you every tried to stand in a canoe? Have you attempted to balance on a rolling log in the water? Without a stable foundation to stand on you cannot rest secure on outcomes of right or wrong. At best, it is right for more than those for whom it is wrong. Can society survive with that level of ambiguity? There comes a time when a person must discover what is right and true and worth pursuing. Those values are based on deep convictions of the soul that require an underpinning stronger than the majority, or the most powerful, or the loudest.

There are times when the right thing to do violates the desire of the majority. Nazi Germany is an example of that. To stand against the status quo requires you to know concretely what you believe. If it isn't based on something other than what humanity can create, it cannot stand against another worldview.

Reflections for the Journey

How do you make decisions or resolve problems? Do you bring your issues to God? What does he say? Knowing the tendency to rely upon strategy to resolve problems, consider your upcoming decisions. Here is an opportunity to bring those issues to God and inquire what he would have you do. Living dependently upon God can only deepen your intimacy with him.

"Only fools say in their hearts, 'There is no God.' They are corrupt, and their actions are evil; not one of them does good (Psalm 14:1)!"

Living in Boxes
Chapter Twenty-three

"He showed you these things so you would know that the Lord is God and there is no other… So remember this and keep it firmly in mind: The Lord is God both in heaven and on earth, and there is no other" (Deuteronomy 4:35–39).

Nineteen-sixty-eight was a strange year. Reports from Vietnam told the sad story of family friends who had been executed. I was angry and wanted to enlist in the American military (as did other Canadians) but age was a restriction.

My church had a good youth group back then. We did a lot together. Most of it was good, some of it wasn't as good. Ironically, whenever we started to do the "not so good" stuff the group would isolate me.

"You can't do this. You're a preacher's kid."

What couldn't I do? These were all friends from the church's youth group. Each one had professed to have committed themselves to obeying the teachings of Jesus the Christ. Now here we all were, together, doing a few things that clearly were not part of a Biblical lifestyle and they came out and said, "We can do it, but you can't."

What box had my life been put in? The only distinguishing difference was that my father was the pastor. The amazing part about this story is that they seemed to honestly believe it.

In reflection it isn't difficult to follow the put-in-a-box rationalization when some are viewed to be in "full-time" Christian service. These are the dedicated few. They become pastors, missionaries, church staff or para-church workers. These are people who have committed 100 percent of their lives to serving God: Full-time Christian Service.

So what were the rest of us? Well, nobody ever said. It was left up to us to decide how full-time we were. In reality, the only expectation for those working in the business community was to attend church functions, to pray and pay.

It isn't a new idea for the Church, nor is it a Biblical one. Can a follower of Jesus the Christ limit his or her commitment? When do we make the decision to follow Christ "part-time"? Yet because of non-verbal communication, a concept has germinated, permitting church goers the latitude to isolate spirituality from business and leisure. It becomes a personal place that does not transgress into life's other areas.

> *It isn't difficult to follow the put-in-a-box rationalization when some are viewed to be in "full-time" Christian service.*

A friend, when asked whether his job was more important for the Kingdom of God than his pastor's, concluded that his pastor's job ultimately was more significant. In reality, that position would be difficult to support from the Bible.

Dualism or Gnosticism, makes that division. It separates the spiritual from the physical; the sacred from the secular. Gnosticism also fails to recognize the deeply spiritual reality found in the wonder of a sunrise. It denies the comfort in our soul by the physical presence of a friend during times of grief and pain. Gnosticism does not realize that God speaks in spiritual ways through natural means. Read through the Bible and discover that God does not recognize the secular. Everything he made is sacred; the visible and the invisible. Every response is either in obedience to him or in resistance to him, nothing more or less.

Reflections for the Journey

Think of how your faith influences your work; how you spend money; how you play? Is faith something that can be separated out from the rest of life?

"Does anybody hear her? Can anybody see?

Or does anybody even know she's going down today?

Under the shadow of our steeple

With all the lost and lonely people

Searching for the hope that's tucked away in you and me

Does anybody hear her? Can anybody see?"

~ John Mark Hall

Consider watching Casting Crowns' music video DVD—*Does Anybody See Her?* www.castingcrowns.com

Perceptions
Chapter Twenty-four

"The problem is not fundamentally hypocrisy. We're all hypocrites at some level. The problem is the air of moral superiority many of us carry around. We stop acknowledging imperfections in our lives. We forget where we came from and all God has done in our lives."
~ David Kinnaman, *UnChristian*

I would love to not be able to give a personal example to this reflection. The truth is, I have struggled with a "better than you" attitude throughout the majority of my life. My only comfort is that I am not alone. With every burst of anger directed towards a person, rather than their behavior, I have come to realize that, at that moment in time, I honestly believe I am better than they are. In that emotional place, I no longer have the capacity to love them as Christ commanded me to love.

In 2007, David Kinnaman's groundbreaking research for the Barna Group explored, "What a new generation really thinks about Christianity and why it matters." (See *UnChristian*.) His findings identified six categories of frustration generally felt towards Christians—Protestant or Catholic—conservative, charismatic and liberal.

Kinnaman identified six perceptions people have of North American Christians:

Hypocritical: saying one thing and doing another; skeptical of our morally superior attitudes.

Too focused on getting converts: feel like targets; question motives.

Anti-homosexual: show disdain for gays and lesbians.

Sheltered: out of touch, old fashioned, simplistic answers and solutions.

Too political: a political agenda promoting conservative interests and issues.

Judgmental: quick to judge; not honest about how they feel about others; doubt they really love them.

It does not matter whether or not these perceptions are accurate. More important is to ask what have we done to leave these impressions upon so many people? The tendency is to defend oneself against accusations we believe to be untrue. Yet that is only important if we have a felt need to position ourselves to be right. In this case, it is more important for society to sense that they have been heard and that we are sorry for coming across in ways that have diminished their value. In taking a posture of humility and love, many of these accusations simply lose credibility.

I have found myself, on numerous occasions, feeling a need to be vindicated. Yet, if I defended myself it would appear that I was hiding something. If I remained silent, then it left the impression that the false statements must be true. Those are lonely places to find oneself. From the midst of that mess grows a strength and tenacity that recognizes the only alternative is to be defended by God himself. Don't be afraid to take up a posture of humble dependency. It is God

> *What have we done to leave these impressions upon so many people?*

who defends the helpless. You may find yourself in a self-made scenario or a vindictive one. Regardless, it is good to seek out the advice of our Sovereign God and resist the knee-jerk reaction.

Reflections for the Journey

Is anger something you struggle with? Whenever our anger is directed towards individuals rather than their behavior, we have moved into a dangerous place. If you were to examine the intent of your heart at that moment, you would discover that you honestly believe you are better than that person.

"Stop being angry! Turn from your rage! Do not lose your temper, it only leads to harm" (Psalm 37:8).

"Fools vent their anger, but the wise quietly hold it back" (Proverbs 29:11).

Self-Interest
Chapter Twenty-five

*If I don't love my neighbor as myself, who do you
suppose I love more?*

Our church had a fundraiser to reduce its debt. Nancy and I didn't have
extra cash but did sense that we needed to participate. It lead us to pray
a simple prayer requesting cash from an unexpected source.

"God, if you will send us some cash, we will give it to the church for its
debt reduction."

That seemed to be a safe prayer. A couple of days later, we received a letter from the city.

"We wish to inform you that you have paid too much municipal tax and
you will be receiving a refund of…"

We had paid too much municipal tax? Who has ever paid too much
municipal tax! Have you ever heard of anyone who has paid too much municipal tax? Income tax maybe, but in my half century, I have never paid too
much municipal tax. My mind started into full gear. With that amount of
money we could address some real needs in our home. We could reduce some
of our debt load; possibly purchase an item on our wish list.

Then came the "still small voice." It's the quiet whisper that says, *That
wasn't the deal.* It was so quiet, I wasn't sure I had heard anything. It
reminded me of my prayer. I decided to put some of the cash towards the

church's debt.

"That wasn't the deal!"

There it was again. This time a little clearer, enough to make me pause and ask, "Did you say something God?"

> If I don't love my
> neighbor as myself,
> who do you suppose
> I love more?

"That wasn't the deal. You're leaving out the 'all' part."

"All? But this is more than I was planning to give."

I'm not sure if the next thought came from God or my own memory, but two names came to mind: Ananias and Sapphira. Have you ever noticed that God doesn't need to be wordy? He has a way about him that is succinct and clear. (Read Acts 5:1–11 if you don't recognize these names.)

It is hard to resist the temptation to constantly add to what we already have. Much of our culture reinforces a sense of entitlement. Rights are championed, but they really aren't the rights of others as much as they are our own rights.

God's invitation to invest in others is not because of his need of our help. It is primarily to help us discover the joy of giving. Self-interest numbs our ability to enjoy life fully. It restricts our perspective of its benefit for us.

Opportunities abound to enjoy life simply because it is wonderful and it has no agenda. Investing in others creates a depth of meaning that cannot be cultivated in any other way. Consider taking time to notice the common, the ordinary, the simplistic, and see if there might be something of greater depth than you have previously realized.

Reflections for the Journey

Is there something that you are holding on to that God is inviting you to give away? What is your point of resistance? What do you fear if it is removed?

———

Read 1 Samuel 25 — The story of Nabul's stubborn-ness, Abigail's discernment and a disaster averted.

Community
Chapter Twenty-six

As God continues his work in us, we become more beautiful to those who are looking.

Jesus spoke about caring for "the least of these." Who are they? There are some marginalized people with whom I enjoy friendship. I don't view them in this category. Maybe "the least of these" are the people I have very little time for. Whoever they are, there was a growing conviction that I needed to begin to intentionally invest in them. Jesus speaks about them (Matthew 25), so I began to ask God for greater understanding.

While attending worldview meetings in Hong Kong, I asked God to help me find one of "the least of these." I didn't know where to find them or what they looked like. I didn't know what to do with them. I simply had a growing longing to care for them and participate in their lives.

Upon my return home, I found a petition in my mailbox, unsigned—from a concerned neighbor. Apparently we had a rehabilitation house in our neighborhood and this individual believed its residents were a danger to our children. It was very much a letter about, "Not in my backyard." The notice provided selected information about this group. I went to the Internet and explored the accusations.

A second, unsigned flier was placed in my mailbox a week later from a concerned neighbor, asking us to join an online petition to have this house removed. They also urged us to go to a meeting at city hall to voice our opposition to this home. In the meantime, we had discovered that this home was operated by Christians. Its policies were based on a discipleship model of education and accountability. The men in this house were behaving responsibly and even came forward and exposed a marijuana grow operation down the street. They were instrumental in having it shut down.

My wife and I determined to attend that meeting. Many opinions were voiced. Many assumptions were shared. Emotion flowed. The men in that house, exposed to the onslaught, felt very little support from their community. The symptoms of veiled prejudice weren't hard to identify.

> *Love is a risk. Love is humbling. Love is not without cost.*

No one had visited these men in their home. No one had seen who lived there and what was done there. No one had offered to help and encourage these men to get off drugs. Almost everyone wanted them to leave our neighborhood. And no one was asking whether this rehabilitation house was part of the problem or part of the solution? These men had shut down a grow op. These men were no longer on the street consuming drugs, and some were no longer stealing cars and breaking into homes. These men had families and wanted their lives back. They felt no encouragement from the neighborhood but they continued on in their commitment to doing the best they could. Imagine the outcome if their neighbors encouraged them, visited them, mentored them.

So I stood in defense of that home. I openly stated I wanted them in our neighborhood. I warned about being careful to not fight part of the solution out of fear. No one wants to place their children at risk. Be wise. Be responsible. Recognize that someone needs to stand and be accounted for. The next day, Nancy made some pastry and we, with our two youngest daughters, went and visited the nine men. They were kind men, good men committed to getting off drugs, wanting to grow in all aspects of their lives, including their spiritual understanding. They had been studying the Bible together but couldn't find anyone to come and guide them.

Love is a risk. Love is humbling. Love is not without cost. But love changes you. It isn't hard to reach out into your own community when it is the byproduct of God's transforming work in your life. It feels very natural. Be careful to not put the cart before the horse. God is transforming you. He does it most effectively as you give yourself to others. Remember Moses' words: *"(Lord) If your presence does not go with us, do not send us from here"* (Ex. 33:15 NIV).

As God continues his work in us, we become more beautiful to those who are looking. We give back to those around us what God has given to us. That includes our knowledge of God (an example being the salvation story). It also includes mercy, grace and justice.

We lost the group housing fight on a technicality. The house was located five meters too close to a public school. The battle, however, for our communities is not over.

Reflections for the Journey

Are you courageous enough to say, "I want the marginalized in my backyard?" Define for yourself who "the least of these" refers to. Seek out those people and find out more about them. Are there ways for you to share parts of your lives with each other? (Read Matthew 25:31–46.)

Authenticity
Chapter Twenty-seven

"And whatever you do, whether in word or deed, do it all in the name of the Lord Jesus, giving thanks to God the Father through him" (Colossians 3:17 NIV).

There is a tension for many of us in knowing how to appropriately respond to people in need. We recognize that we have resources. We have a sense of responsibility, but we don't necessarily know where to begin. We want to care. Are there risks? Probably. Do we want to be humbled? Maybe.

As a young father, I was conscious of how impressionable my children were. My four-year-old daughter was sitting on my lap as I watched TV. The show was somewhat violent for a young child so I scooted her off, sending her out of the room with these words: "Melody, this isn't a good show for you to watch. It's too violent."

About 10 minutes later, I heard a voice from behind my chair. It said, "Papa, if this show isn't good for me to watch, isn't good for you to watch it either." Ouch!

A mature man would have simply said, "You are absolutely right," and turned off the TV. That is what a mature man would have done. I, on the other hand, started into my mental rationalization of why this show was fine for me to watch. After all, how bad can *The A Team* be? It required an extended moment before my love for my daughter took the upper hand.

Possibly one of the greatest deterrents to authenticity is humanity's propensity to rationalize away personal responsibility. If we can convince ourselves that we are not responsible, then we are free to not be accountable. Authenticity, on the other hand, welcomes accountability. It sees it as a friend that assists us in living what we say. Jesus directed us to this place. He said, "Simply let your 'Yes' be 'Yes', and your 'No,' 'No'; anything beyond this comes from the evil one" (Matthew 5:37 paraphrased).

Paul gave the same type of warning to slaves who had become followers of Jesus the Christ.

"Slaves, obey your earthly masters in everything; and do it, not only when their eye is on you and to win their favor, but with sincerity of heart and reverence for the Lord. Whatever you do, work at it with all your heart, as working for the Lord, not for men..." (Colossians 3:22–23 NIV).

> *One of the greatest deterrents to authenticity is humanity's propensity to rationalize away personal responsibility*

My children often ask me for favors. When I would accomodate, they continued to ask, "Do you promise?" It didn't take me long to realize they shouldn't have to ask me that question. I have made it my practice to follow through on what I have said. I want to be known as a person whose word is as good as his bond. They know now that I don't need to promise if I say I will do it.

Reflections for the Journey

How well do you follow through on the commitments you make? Does the quality of your work change when you are being supervised by someone else?

———•••••———

"Vanity it is, to wish to live long, and to be careless to live well."

~ Thomas à Kempis, *The Imitation of Christ*

———•••••———

"The world is evil only when you become its slave. The world has a lot to offer – just don't feel bound to obey it."

~ Henri Nouwen, *Life of the Beloved*

Presence
Chapter Twenty-eight

We can only reflect what we expose ourselves to.

I looked into the eyes of Christina Noble—a feisty little Irish lady—a woman who was raised on the street—a woman who knew hunger and would pretend that the folded leaves in her hand were in fact a sandwich, and she would eat them—a woman who was gang raped as a teen and experienced abuse for most of her life. I looked into those eyes and listened to a scathing rebuke of humanity that would allow pedophiles to propagate on the streets of Vietnam and other countries.

I listened as she cursed the Westerner who enticed a little ten-year-old girl to his room. I recoiled when hearing the horrors of the street—of nursing babies suckling on genitals; of beaten and battered children. I saw the caved-in faces, the swollen and bruised ears that no longer heard, I saw the shattered souls of children who had been convinced that they were somehow to blame for the unspeakable injustice that had tortured their little lives—and I cry out to God—Oh God, how long?

How long will the Church be impotent—how long will we refuse to stretch our hands out to the helpless—how long will we value things more than life? How long will we target the poor with mission strategies that were designed for middle-upper class society and rationalize away their lack of response as being hardness of heart? How long?

At times it feels like I have seen too much. It gets muddled in my mind and becomes difficult to process. Serving others is one of the most effective introductions a person can receive to a living and loving God. We never stop serving, because it is our life. Through living fully, we reflect the glory of God into our community for all to see.

The Apostle Paul described us as individuals who reflect the glory of God wherever we go (2 Corinthians 3:17–18). He placed the emphasis on the transformation of God in our lives

> *We are merely reflections of the glory of God.*

rather than on our own accomplishments or our carefully crafted apologetics. This does not negate the importance of being willing to explain to people what we honestly believe. It does, however, remove the responsibility for the results of our conversations.

We are merely reflections of the glory of God. We can only reflect what we expose ourselves to. Moses understood the implications when he said, "Lord, if your Presence does not go with us, what will distinguish us from anyone else."

The underlying issue that each of us must face is whether we are moving to the rhythm of God's heart beat. You may very well have logically worked out a course of action for your life and are pursuing that plan. It is worthwhile to take the time to examine whether it has anything to do with God's story and his plan, with caring for our world.

The greatest gift to an orphaned child is loving presence.

Reflections for the Journey

What is your understanding of God's agenda for your community? When it comes to your community, how do you fit into God's agenda?

———•·•·•———

"Neither do people light a lamp and put it under a bowl. Instead, they put it on its stand, and it gives light to everyone in the house. In the same way, let your light shine before men, that they may see your good deeds and praise your Father in heaven"
(Matthew 5:15–17 NIV).

Sin
Chapter Twenty-nine

Some fear it. Others embellish it. What is it?

My wife and I were sent out as missionaries in the late 1980s. Our assignment was to help start new churches by evangelizing and then teaching converts about their new-found faith. The location, however, was refugee camps in Thailand and the Philippines. We lived on a cost-of-living allowance. We had a budget for the assignment. We did not have a budget for the obvious needs of the refugees we encountered.

Daily, we had to make decisions from our own food supply when the needy would come to our door.

Weekly, we chose to purchase medicine for sick babies and ensure it was administered rather than sold on the black market by a desperate mother.

Hourly, we listened to horrific stories of wounded, broken people and we knew we had to help.

We had no money, no formal mandate and no experience. From those ashes came vocational training classes, counseling, advocacy and friendship.

Upon our return to North America, I was asked on three different occasions if I would consider starting up Food for the Hungry in Canada. Each time, I said, "No", until I began to wonder if possibly God was behind the invitation.

Reflections

It launched a personal quest to understand what God had to say about the needy and the broken. I had received extensive training regarding the wellbeing of a person's soul. I had received no formal training regarding a person's health and dignity.

It led me to extend my time of personal study in the Bible. In that context I discovered an expanded explanation of another ugly story. This time it was found in the book of Genesis rather than a refugee camp.

The story of Sodom and Gomorra is a graphic story. Abraham's herdsmen were fighting with the herdsmen of his nephew Lot. Not wanting the internal bickering to break up his family, Abraham allowed Lot to graze his herds on the fertile plains of Sodom and Gomorra.

Years later, God visited Abraham and informed him that he was going down to Sodom. Instinctively, Abraham's first response was, "You won't destroy Sodom if there are 50 righteous people living there will you? How about 45, 40, 30, 20, 10?"

> *Pride, self-indulgence, and indifference led them to an inability to see the needs of people around them.*

Why did God destroy these cities? It would be worthwhile to read the Genesis account. Chapters 18–19 describe a city where its men were attempting to rape two visitors and a father who was willing to offer his two virgin daughters to be raped in order to protect his guests. Clearly, it was a sanitized version of events but graphic enough just the same.

Ezekiel 16:49 (NIV) reveals a deeper motive: *"Now this was the sin of your sister Sodom: She and her daughters were arrogant, overfed and unconcerned; they did not help the poor and needy."*

Pride, self-indulgence, and indifference led them to an inability to see the needs of people around them.

The visual detail of the Genesis story describes the symptoms of a deeper issue. Ezekiel is describing the cause—the root—the source for the conduct described in Genesis.

Symptoms are easy to see. They consume our emotions and responses while far too little thought is given to identifying the reasons behind behavior. The cause of the tragedy in Sodom was arrogance, self-indulgence and indifference. It allowed the citizens of that city to pursue whatever ends they desired without moral restraint or accountability.

The implications of this story challenge the root issues of our lives. When we do not make the effort to examine our motives, we easily fall prey to our own arrogance, self-indulgence, and indifference, accompanied by a complete lack of compassion. Freedom without restraint is bondage. The protection of rights without responsibility become tyrannical.

Reflections for the Journey

What causes am I prepared to defend? If this is the only type of intervention, will this problem ever go away? What has caused this problem to evolve? How has arrogance, self-indulgence and indifference assisted in the evolution of this issue?

"For the wages of sin is death, but the free gift of God is eternal life through Christ Jesus our Lord" (Romans 6:23).

Value
Chapter Thirty

"One of the most significant ways to serve others is to be present with them."
~ Charles Ringma, *Dare to Journey with Henri Nouwen*

No one credible ever told me that I needed to grow up. Deep longings in my soul to be cherished were never fully met. My son experienced the same depths of despair. He voiced it one day in an effort to please me.

"Am I being a good sport dad?"

He was asking me if he "measured up". He spoke my words. "Am I good enough yet?"

"Will you like me now?"

"Will I be your cherished son now?"

These words are not directed towards my father. They are simply spoken from the heart of a child in a man's body. A child who had not had enough cherishing in his life to know that he was special, that he was loved and that he had nothing he needed to prove.

Value is a word of association. Does an item have value if there is no cost associated with it? Is there value with nothing to compare it to?

Gold—hunting for it is a favorite pastime. I have moved small mountains

PRICELESS WORKS OF ART

looking for it. Wrenching on a crowbar, an intense pain shot through my chest; not a good place for a heart attack. My dilemma: Should I go straight to the hospital and risk losing my panning gear, or haul out the gear and die in the process? The risk was worth it. I hauled all my gear back out of the woods and drove myself to emergency. I had popped a rib.

Why do I expend such a tremendous amount of physical exertion, willingly working in isolation, facing the elements with little hope of discovering anything of significance? Many reasons, but once I uncovered a nugget.

I was up to my waist in a swift moving, icy mountain river. I had discovered a clay bar midstream. Digging deep, I worked through seven pans without even a trace of gold. It led to a running dialogue with God that sounded something like: "You could help out you know. It's not as though I'm trying to get something for nothing. Money is tight right now and this could really help."

Determined this was the last pan if I didn't find anything, I balanced my shovel and, with numb fingers, prepared to work the gravel. This time, though, I could see a little yellow stone on the surface of the pan. I remember thinking, "Isn't this just like you God, to throw a piece of yellow clay on top just as I am having this dialogue with you."

I decided to pick that one stone out and throw it away so that it wouldn't distract the cleaning process. As I lifted

> *Does an item have value if there is no cost associated with it?*

it to toss it back into the stream, I noticed the weight and took a closer look.

"Holy cow! Isn't that just like you God. Just when I start whining about you not stepping in, you lay a nugget right on the top of my pan."

Seven more pans produced absolutely nothing. Body aching, I sat in my cabin that night, eating straight out of a can of cold beans with the nugget lying on the table. I listened to the lyrics from the song, *When It's All Been Said and Done*. "You find purest gold in miry clay, turning sinners into saints."

And God seemed to audibly say, *"See that nugget? That's what's in you. You are miry clay filled with gold and I am refining it out of you."*

"Isn't that just like you God! After I whine about how you could be helping me out of some financial hardships, you drop a nugget into my pan. Then you turn it into a symbolic representation of my life that is so significant, I can't sell it!"

Reflections for the Journey

From the following list, identify the most valuable/significant factor in each category: friend, personal pursuit, possession, time consumer. What is the most significant aspect that gives each value?

———•◦•◦•———

"Wherever your treasure is, there the desires of your heart will also be" (Matthew 6:21).

Hope
Chapter Thirty-one

The humble poor know a deep secret. They give from themselves, not from their surplus. They give from the abundance of their hearts.
   ~ Kefa Sampangi, *A Distant Grief*

Kefa Sempangi wrote about an African proverb that says:

Giving flows from a good spirit as a river flows to the lake. It is not a matter of possessions. The river can never give back to its source, what it has taken. It simply passes on its water to the lake, even though the waters of the lake are many times greater... There is a giving to serve others and there is a giving to serve oneself. There is a giving to promote, and a giving to dominate. Without love there is only paternalism and self-importance. There is only the giving of surplus, not the giving of precious treasures.
   ~ *A Distant Grief* (out of print)

I sat on a six-inch stool in a side alley. It was dark. Night had come to Saigon. Across from me was a young woman. Her little baby lay listless in her arms. Beside me stood her four-year-old daughter, eyes twinkling in the light. I drew the little girl onto my knee and she happily complied. Her mother's face bore the strain of life on the street. They were heavy and weary—tired of the battle, yet determined to plod on. Another step, another day that will bring the same as the last. Where does she find bread for her child?

The three bowls of soup I ordered were placed in front of us. The third bowl was for an obnoxious man—pushy and abrasive from the hardness of life. Clearly, this little mother barely tolerated his presence.

I turned back to the woman. I knew that the solution for her was not so impossible and yet it would probably never happen. All she would need was to have someone come along side, invest, at most, $100, walk her through the initial steps of running a little street business of selling soup—the same as we were eating there on the sidewalk.

> *Sustainable solutions begin with inspiring hope.*

But such simple solutions require people. There were no people. There was no money. And I looked into this mother's eyes and realized she had no hope.

The soul is the place of deepest communion with our Creator. When the longing simply is not there, we are invited to ask God to create it. As he draws us to himself, we identify with his love. His love for the marginalized creates a longing within us to build relationships with them.

Sustainable solutions begin with inspiring hope. Without hope, "people perish." It is true; hope is readily visible to those who have eyes to see it. In developing communities, the level of hope can be quickly measured using three visual clues. First, how much garbage is lying on the ground? People with hope don't leave garbage. Second, how well are the buildings maintained? People with hope paint, repair and maintain infrastructure. Third, are there planted flowers? People with hope take time for aesthetics.

Jesus Christ's message was given to instill hope. We in turn, invest wisely in our communities when we desire to see healing and wholeness take place at the root levels of despair.

Hope provides a vision of where we are going. It helps to reframe the past so that we are okay with it, and enables us to make small, good and wise decisions in the present. The goal is to create small successes. If we can even take the smallest step and recognize it as one step toward our goal, we have something to celebrate. Over time, hope begins to grow.

Reflections for the Journey

What would make you glad to wake up in the morning? What makes that such a powerful encouragement to you? Hope is a way of helping people do things in a different way so that they can achieve a different result. The process may be slow but as we help people do well on one assignment or task it allows them to move forward, one success at a time.

"There can only be two basic loves. The love of God unto the forgetfulness of self, or the love of self unto the forgetfulness and denial of God."
~ Augustine

"And whatever you do or say, do as a representative of the Lord Jesus, giving thanks through him to God the Father" (Colossians 3:17).

"My hope is built on nothing less than Jesus' blood and righteousness... On Christ the solid rock I stand; all other ground is sinking sand."
~ Edward Mote (1797–1874)

Change
Chapter Thirty-two

Change is the place where I discover who I really am.

I sat in my office, knowing that I simply could not go on. I was through, wasted, spent. Anticipating another year in my current position was similar to shaking an already empty cup, trying to get that last drop adhered to the bottom to fall. This had been all I ever wanted to do. It was what I fully intended to do until I died. Now, if I continued on, I knew I would die a whole lot sooner than I wanted to.

But what does a person do when they know they cannot stay in the position that was supposed to last a lifetime? What are the options when no other possibilities have ever been considered?

It is such a small word. Its implications can be unsettling. Some seek it, but most find themselves confronted by it. At times we have the luxury of preparing for it. The worst form of change occurs when the freight train slams into your life at 80 miles an hour and you didn't see it coming: a lost job, a death, a betrayal, a confession.

Change can also include making peace with your past. Life holds some of us hostage in a time when Jesus pronounced that he came to set the captive free.

Some are more willing to stay with the abuse than risk the fear of the unknown or untested. Others are caught when life itself seems to be slipping away at too fast a rate—a midlife crisis, a sense of urgency for something more, something different—a change.

We can pursue it with reckless abandon simply for its own sake. It is also possible to lay it aside and pursue God instead. In a willingness to release all things sacred to him, to put everything on the table and be open for anything, it is possible to discover new horizons that you have never considered. Sometimes they are most clearly seen when we look back and view where we have come.

At its heart though, change should be nothing more than our willingness to obey God. It is not meant to be its own destination. It is a byproduct of listening to guidance from our source of knowledge, the One who knows more than we can comprehend.

It is written: *"No eye has seen, no ear has heard, no mind has conceived what God has prepared for those who love him"* (1Cor. 2:9 NIV).

That level of confidence enables us to trust that each circumstance that crosses our path can move us one step closer to experiencing something we never dreamt possible. In times when everything around us seems to be shifting, Christ is pictured as our rock, our foundation, immovable, unchangeable, steady, dependable God.

> *Change should be nothing more than our willingness to obey God.*

Reflections for the Journey

Do you struggle with pessimism? What would a positive future look like for you? What steps would move you closer to your dream?

Ask God what he is willing to do about the things you are concerned about.

———•••———

"Give your burdens to the Lord, and he will take care of you. He will not permit the godly to slip and fall"
(Psalm 55:22).

Devotion
Chapter Thirty-three

Service is simply about serving. It isn't about fairness. It isn't about return. It is about emptying oneself so there are fewer things that distract.

Jesus, on his final trip to Jerusalem, was invited into the home of Martha, sister of Mary. Martha busied herself with the preparations for a meal while Mary sat at Jesus' feet and listened to him. Martha became indignant at Mary's unwillingness to help. She implored Jesus to tell Mary to do her part. Jesus response was, *"Martha, Martha, you are worried and upset about many things, but only one thing is needed. Mary has chosen what is better, and it will not be taken away from her"* (Lk.10:41–42 NIV).

The truth is, I have been a Martha most of my life. I have struggled with sitting and "doing" nothing. It has been a challenge for me to meditate without movement. I like to think while I work. I think and process in conversation with others. For years I would take on a project, play a game, do anything, rather than sit and read. The one exception was a good novel if it carried me to other worlds that absorbed my imagination.

So, naturally, a quiet devotional time was an act of discipline. Journaling required great effort. I empathize with Martha. There was work that needed to be done.

If no meal was prepared, would everyone be so gracious about having only a diet of teaching? Is there not a balance between activity and inactivity, between responsibility and devotion? Is it acceptable to ask others to assume the responsibility for work that is yours, so that you can have more time to reflect in devotion with God? At what point do the needs of others carry priority over personal growth and worship? Cannot work be a form of worship in itself? Does personal devotion require the neglect of other responsibilities?

Martha was frustrated with Mary, and rightly so. Yet Jesus heightens the tension by siding with Mary; Lazy Mary. So what is the point? Is this just an issue of personality traits? Some are more task orientated than others? That probably plays some part in the frustration.

The part I don't want to acknowledge is that it shouldn't matter to me. Why am I bothered by Mary's actions and Jesus' response? I run the risk of not getting credit when doing things for others.

Service eliminates the gods in a person's life and allows you to love someone else to the point of permitting them to be filled up while you are being emptied.

> *At what point do the needs of others carry priority over personal growth and worship?*

There are times when we need to be replenished and times when we need to be emptied. Mary was thirsty for inner renewal. She was taken up by the majesty of her guest. She wanted to hear from him, to learn from him, to worship him. Martha, on the other hand, wanted to honor him by doing something for him. She didn't want to do it for Mary. It was one thing to do it for an honored and deserving guest. It was quite another thing to do it for a lazy sister. And there it lies in all its ugliness. Martha's desire to give was connected to her need to receive. She wanted her efforts to be recognized. She had done something that was worthy of praise. She wanted Jesus' acknowledgement and thanks for all that she did for him. It was something that was due her. She didn't need a sister's thanks. Her motive for serving was to receive in return.

Mary sat at the feet of Jesus and offered nothing. She simply took in. Her actions were that of a child. Yet she was getting all of Jesus' attention. Martha was the one who had invited Jesus home. Jesus was her guest, not Mary's. But little Mary steps up and ignores Martha's needs and monopolizes Jesus. Martha is doing all the work and receiving no attention. Mary is doing none of the work and receiving all the attention.

Jesus' words were simply, "Mary wants me, not my praise or acknowledgement. It is a better thing and I am going to make sure she receives that."

Reflections for the Journey

Do I want Jesus more than his praise?

"O God, you are my God;
I earnestly search for you.
My soul thirsts for you;
my whole body longs for you
in this parched and weary land
where there is no water"
(Psalm 63:1).

Justice
Chapter Thirty-four

"The way you are with others every day, regardless of their status, is the true test of faith."
~ Brennan Manning

Look around. Feel a little overwhelmed at times? I listened to a talk show where callers vented. Their basic message was, "Not in my backyard."

We lost the fight to keep our rehabilitation house in our neighborhood. Closed down on a technicality. It was five meters too close to a school. Five meters. Nine lives.

When justice is undermined and injustice upheld—when evil has greater influence than good—then the foundations of the earth are undermined. When the sustaining principles of God are compromised, earth becomes vulnerable. The "glue" breaks down.

"God (Elohim) stands in the divine assembly. With him are his appointed elohim (judges). There he pronounces judgment.

How long will you judge unfairly?

You favor the wicked.

Give justice to the vulnerable.

Uphold their rights

Rescue them

Deliver/protect them from the exploitation of the wicked" (Psalms 82:1–4 Complete Jewish Bible).

God's judgment begins with a statement and charge: "You are all elohim. You cannot blame others for your dereliction of responsibility. You are responsible for both the mess and the solution. The solution is found in how you treat the vulnerable and how you call to account those who exploit."

> *When justice is undermined and injustice upheld then the foundations of the earth are undermined.*

Life, at times, asks if we are prepared to take that stand. Rise up Elohim(God). This earth and its nations are yours. Elohim, raise up elohim(judges) to guard against the temptation of power and possessions.

Reflections for the Journey

What do you see when you encounter a street person? What do you say to the single mother? What do you offer the low income family. Our time can be more valuable than our money.

"O people, the Lord has told you what is good, and this is what he requires of you: to do what is right, to love mercy, and to walk humbly with your God" (Micah 6:8).

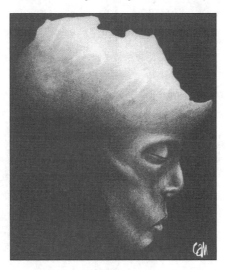

More
Chapter Thirty-five

"Doing more for God is the method servants use to increase in favor. A friend has a different focus entirely. They enjoy the favor they have and use it to spend time with their friend."
~ Bill Johnson, *Dreaming With God*

Something is going on inside of me. Maybe it's gaining clarity, but I find myself wanting more of it.

I have pursued "more" through education. Bible school and seminary taught me much about God and some of it was simply wrong. I pursued "more" through serving. I was taught a variety of methods. "Do you want to know God? Try this…"

I became a pastor, a counselor, a missionary, a humanitarian. Some of that was simply life choices. Some of it was fulfilling the assumed expectations of others. And some of it was simply my own need to know more of God.

I am old enough to have transitioned through almost every stage of television technology. Black and white with limited stations and hours; the tube; flat panel; high def; Blue Ray 3D (don't own that one but have seen it). The picture and experience gets better and better. No matter how profound the experience, I remain a spectator. I can enter in but am still not a part. It parallels my faith. I recognize that the longing and the drawing I am experiencing is to become part of the screenplay.

How can a person be drawn into life and breath interaction with Jesus? When can we distinguish between speaking about the authority of the Christ and speaking his authority? When does petition move to dialogue?

Jesus made a distinction between servants and friends. The invitation was to friendship. I have thought about the difference. How would my treatment of a servant, assuming I was the best of masters, differ from my relationship with a friend? (Read John 15:15.)

> *Much more will be done by the person who is responding because of love than the one who is acting out of duty.*

Clearly, friendship carries with it a greater level for freedom, entitlement and a different set of expectations. Friendship relies heavily upon desire where "servanthood" rests on control. Yet the posture of a servant is so frequently seen within Christendom. Jesus himself took up a towel and washed feet. Yet the profoundness of that act is only recognized when you realize that he was not required to do it. He chose to do it out of love.

Have I carried the wrong idea of servanthood into my faith journey?

I have friends who tell me that we need the "Marthas" of the Bible. Martha was Mary's sister, who was doing all the work while Mary sat and listened to Jesus. My friends tell me that without "Marthas," nothing would get done. So why does Jesus say that Mary has chosen the better thing (Luke 10:38–42)? It simply isn't true that "Marys" do not work. I would suggest to you that the "Marys" of this world are the ones who have discovered the role of friend and the "Marthas" still see themselves as servants. Marys are the Mother Theresas. Marthas are the keepers of the institution. They fulfill a job, a role, an obligation.

Much more will be done by the person who is responding because of love than the one who is acting out of duty. Love trumps duty.

It is interesting though to have experienced so much resistance from friends on this very point. I have come to believe that they have a very difficult time trusting love. It can't be controlled. It can't be demanded. It is therefore impossible to predict and we do not have authority over it to force it to conform. Because its starting point is love and not duty, it cannot be forced. Once it responds based on coercion, it is no longer an act of love. It is an act of duty performed by a servant, not a friend.

The difference between the two is that one finds himself as a spectator and the other in the screenplay. You may have the latest technology but it still leaves you the observer. Somewhere there is a place of discovery in our faith, when realization comes and surrender is more complete. It is difficult to rest in the truth that we are loved, that we are friends, intimate with God and he with us. Yet faith is being part of the cast. The most minute role is more engaging than observation using the most sophisticated technology.

Reflections for the Journey

What would healthy control look like in your local church?

"More about Jesus would I know,
More of His grace to others show,
More of His saving fullness see,
More of His love who died for me
...More about Jesus let me learn,
More of His holy will discern;
Spirit of God, my teacher be,
Showing the things of Christ to me."
~ Eliza E. Hewitt (1851–1920)

"As the deer pants for streams of water,
so I long for you, O God.
I thirst for God, the living God.
When can I come and stand before him"
(Psalm 42:1–2).

Abundance
Chapter Thirty-six

"Perhaps of all my many sins toward heaven, this ranks as the worst. I have never thanked God for a single leaf. Which is the problem with faithfulness. We hardly notice it... We live amidst surpassing wonders but most of it has become 'run of the mill'."
~ Mark Buchanan

Jesus said that he came "that we might have life and have it abundantly." Heaven is good, but it is difficult to imagine. Today can be good but that fact can be lost if we simply diminish salvation's impact to our status in eternity.

Jesus said, "Take my yoke on you. For my yoke is easy and my burden is light."

But God, the burden has seemed heavy for a significant portion of my life and life has its way of chafing and rubbing me raw. The yoke hurts my shoulders.

Somewhere in the invitation is the gentle rebuke. "If your burden is heavy and the yoke of life is leaving open wounds on your body, you are carrying something that belongs to God."

I began a closer examination of my life, my experiences and, most importantly, my motives.

The Kingdom of God is like a treasure for which you would sell all that you have to possess it. The Kingdom of God is like the smallest of seeds that grows large and provides shelter for the birds of the air. The Kingdom of God is like yeast, once mixed into dough, permeates it all.

The Kingdom of God affects all of your life. It permeates all of your being. It is worth all that you possess.

> *The Kingdom of God is like yeast, once mixed into dough, permeates it all.*

Imagine living that way.

It is a treasure waiting to be discovered. As I recover it, it consumes my longings. It spreads by itself through every part of me. I want it.

That is very different from my life experience. There have been moments of passion and years of plodding on. There has been guilt, denial of some dreams, lists of requirements, expectations of others to bend me into conformity. Most of it had nothing to do with God, but I thought it did.

The mystery occurs when God draws us into something deeper. Experience may tell you its anticipated answer. God invites you to resist defaulting to those positions too quickly. There is so much we simply do not understand or even know about. Life is more fulfilling when it is approached with a heart that is open to anything that God may steer your way.

Jesus' point was simple. He came to give us life and to restore all things to their intended place. Religion tends to corrupt that message with a counterfeit of striving and denial. Be careful to examine what you are surrendering to. This intimacy with God tunes your hearing to the voice of God and releases you from needing to imitate his offer.

We had no idea that we could be set free from addictions; that we could honestly release the guilt and hate from our past; that we could begin to let go of our striving and trust his ability to recondition our attitudes and desires.

I was raised on a diet of salvation from hell. Now I have added to it, salvation from striving.

Reflections for the Journey

When you think about abundance, what do you desire? If you could ask God for anything, what would it be? What restrictions exist in your life and how do they measure up against this idea of freedom and the mystery of treasure?

"This is what the Lord says—the Lord who made the earth, who formed and established it, whose name is the Lord: Ask me and I will tell you remarkable secrets you do not know, about things to come" (Jeremiah 33:2–3).

Longings
Chapter Thirty-seven

"Our dreams are not independent from God,
but instead, exist because of God."
~ Bill Johnson, *Dreaming With God*

As a child, I used to dream that I had a million dollars to give away. I would itemize the disbursement and then enjoy the pretending. Yet that was the extent of the fantasy. I kept it tucked away in the "dream" category of my life. How would I ever possess so much cash that I could give away a million dollars?

Mine is a charmed life. When I founded an international charity, that childhood dream had not been factored in. Years later, God seemed to remind me of that little child and he showed me how he had allowed that dream to come true. Millions of dollars every year were invested in the lives of deserving people. It was one of the great privileges of my life.

As an adult, I longed for a vocation that would allow me to not only live out my faith, but also to be mentored in my faith. For the last twenty years, God has used refugee camps, political wrangling, injustice, violence, greed, and indifference to shape the person I am becoming. He is answering the "why?" question. He is proving his faithfulness and supply. As I grow closer to God, I am stopping to reflect on what my heart longs for now.

David was king in Israel. He had a remarkable faith: simple, trusting, honest. He was so authentic that God even declared him a man after God's own heart. He was incredibly flawed. He wasn't exactly a role-model father. He lusted. He murdered. He shirked his responsibility. At a time when kings went to war, David sent his army off without him.

Yet when he repented, it was genuine, deeply penetrating his soul. He cried out to God. He was a master at lament. And he had one great longing in his heart. He wanted to build God a temple. That was the one dream that he was not allowed to complete, but he was allowed to start by collecting all the needed materials. Solomon, his son, would be the one to build the temple. That is the context for Solomon's declaration.

> *As our hearts long to know God, God allows himself to be known.*

God said, "I have not chosen a city in any tribe of Israel to have a temple built for my Name… but I have chosen David to rule. The LORD said to my father David, 'Because it was in your heart to build a temple for my Name…'" God willingly met Israel there. The implication is that God was not only aware of David's heart, he chose to honor his longing because his longing was to honor God.

As our hearts long to know God, God allows himself to be known. The more that we come to know God, the greater our longing to bless him. He allows us to dream. He allows you to set those dreams in motion towards reality. He even allows us to discover him more intimately as we pursue the dreams of our souls. It is most gratifying to witness those same dreams become reality.

Reflections for the Journey

Pay attention to the dreams and longings you have in life. Pursue them.

"Since the day I brought my people Israel out of Egypt, I have not chosen a city … but I have chosen David… But the LORD said to my father David, 'Because it was in your heart to build a temple for my Name, you did well…" (1 Kings 8:16–20, 27–30 NIV).

Holiness
Chapter Thirty-eight

Every moment of your life is an encounter with God.

I have wondered what holiness is. Sometimes I defined it as my best effort. Other times it personifies God. Just when it appeared to be taking root in my life, I seemed to do something that confirmed I have a long way still to go. Holiness.

I sat in a small thatched home in remote northern Laos. The village chief wished to expressed his gratitude for the abundance of food we had enabled them to produce each year. It was a primitive place in many ways. Yet there I sat on the bamboo floor as they celebrated the bounty of their lives. For me to live in those conditions would have seemed like the worst of personal poverty. I recognized that if they knew what I knew, if they understood the lifestyle that I have been blessed to live, they could never be content again.

Almost as though God was reading my thoughts, an image came vividly to mind. There were about seven angels sitting around a glimmering pond in heaven. They were laughing and slapping each other in fits of hysterics. They kept pointing into that translucent pond.

I was carried above them and able to look deep into that pond to see what they were laughing at. I could see me sitting in that same thatched hut. I could hear the angels as they said, "If he knew, what we knew, he would never be content again."

Reflections

The simplest descriptor of holiness is God. He is the definition. He lives it. We're told that in him there is no sin at all. The Maker has the right to set the rules. Does that sound oppressive?

Shake the fist, rant a little. Talk about how that's not fair. Yet what if the pursuit of holiness increased your sense of meaning and purpose? What if holiness opened a door to you that increased your fulfillment and provided you with inner peace and joy, patience, kindness, gentleness and love, goodness, self-control...? Would you want it? Would it still seem unfair to you?

> *The holiness demanded by God is only possible through God.*

Holiness falls into the category of, "You don't know what you don't know." Demanding it seems so easy to criticize yet it also seems to be part of the hidden treasure we are told is discovered as we explore the Kingdom of God.

It seems to take so much effort. It's hard being holy. The good news is the fact that we can't produce it. The holiness demanded by God is only possible through God.

"For God is working in you, giving you the desire and the power to do what pleases him" (Philippians 2:13).

Every moment of our lives is an encounter with God. Whether you are struggling in an awkward environment at work or walking along glacier-fed streams in the mountain foothills, the reality is that the Creator is with you. How I respond to his creation is going to depend on what I honestly believe about him. When I walk closely with God, it becomes more difficult to ignore injustice and poverty. How I handle and steward the environment is also influenced by my realization that he created it and it still belongs to him. If I love him, I will strive to love what he loves.

Holiness works itself out in our lifestyle. Yet holiness is primarily the attitude within my soul. Too many years have been spent discovering that holiness is not measured by my behavior. It is measured by my motive and my place of dependency.

Holiness enables me to begin to think the thoughts of God, to see his heart and know his will. It is the reason for my own existence. It is a homecoming. It is not just about what I escape from. It is the discovery of my purpose for life. It is God's transforming work in me so that I more accurately reflect his image in my life.

Reflections for the Journey

When you think about holiness, what comes to mind first: behavior or attitude?

Bibliography
Resouces for the Journey

Dave Andrews, *Compassionate Community Work*, Piquant Editions, 2006

Mark Buchanan, *The Rest of God*, W Publishing Group, 2006

Michael Card, *A Sacred Sorrow*, NavPress, 2005

Casting Crowns DVD – *Does Anybody See Her?* www.castingcrowns.com

Malcolm Gladwell, *Blink: The Power of Thinking Without Thinking*, Little, Brown & Co., 2005

Mike Goheen, *The Gospel & Globalization*, Regent Pub., 2009

Brad Jersak, *Kissing the Leper*, Fresh Wind Press, 2006

Bill Johnson, *Dreaming With God*, Destiny Image Pub., 2006

Brennan Manning, *Abba's Child*, NavPress, 2002

Darrow Miller, *Discipling Nations*, YWAM Publishing, 2001

Bob Moffat, *If Jesus Were Mayor*, Monarch Books, 2006

Bryant Myers, *Walking With The Poor*, Orbis Books, 1999

Henri Nouwen, *Life of the Beloved*, Crossroad Pub. Co., 1992

Kefa Sempangi, *A Distant Grief* (Out of print)

A. W. Tozer, *Knowledge of the Holy*, HarperCollins Pub. Inc., 1961

Philip Yancey, *Disappointment With God*, Zondervan, 1988

William Young, *The Shack,* Windblown Media, 2007

About the Author

David Collins is the son of missionary parents. Raised in Vietnam, David has committed much of his life to helping those less fortunate. He has founded several organizations including Canadian Food for the Hungry International, the Global Hunger Foundation and Paradigm Ministries. David's longing is to create sacred space for worldview dreamers to discover the missing pieces.

David views the Church, God's people, as a primary vehicle for bringing reconciliation and wholeness to a world that has lost its way. For that to happen however, the Church must change.

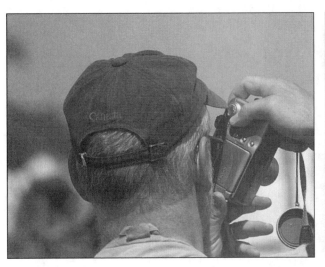

David is married to Nancy, his childhood girlfriend. Together they have 4 children. They have lived throughout Asia and David has traveled extensively across the globe, primarily to regions broken by war, economic and natural disasters. David's firm conviction is that the answer for the needs of the world lies in the application of the Kingdom of God on Earth, the only sustainable solution.

He is a guest lecturer, consultant for church and Christian school boards, a teacher and coach with a pastor's heart. For more specific information, you can visit www.paradigmministries.ca.